UNSPOKEN LOVE

An Orphan's Journey

Jack McCabe

BOOKSIDE Press

Copyright © 2023 by Jack McCabe

ISBN: 978-1-77883-093-8 (Paperback)

All rights reserved. No part of this publication may be reproduced, distributed, or transmitted in any form or by any means, including photocopying, recording, or other electronic or mechanical methods, without the prior written permission of the publisher, except in the case brief quotations embodied in critical reviews and other noncommercial uses permitted by copyright law.

The views expressed in this book are solely those of the author and do not necessarily reflect the views of the publisher, and the publisher hereby disclaims any responsibility for them. Some names and identifying details in this book have been changed to protect the privacy of individuals.

BookSide Press
877-741-8091
www.booksidepress.com
orders@booksidepress.com

Contents

Dedication..V
Ominous Beginnings...2
Early Orphanage Life..12
Becoming a Teenager...34
A Road Trip..58
My First Enlistment..68
My Second Enlistment...78
An Island in the Pacific..90
An Honorable Discharge......................................102
Success and Failure...112
Searching for My Parents.....................................118
A Life with Mathematics......................................124
The Beginning of Thornwell Orphanage.............128
Reflections..130
A Letter to My Great Granddaughter...................134
About the Author..144
Appendix...146

Dedication

I dedicate this book to the memory of my brother, Gordon (Buster) C. McCabe, and to the memory of my brother-in law, Richard C. Hawkins. Their love was most often unspoken; their timely actions of support and guidance spoke loudly. Their trust and encouragement made all the difference for me as I attempted to recover from the mistakes of my youth.

Ominous Beginnings

'Life is a succession of lessons which must be lived to be understood.' —Helen Keller

It was 1953; I was seventeen and already a thief. I was sitting on a Greyhound bus, hoping to get away from a town in northeast Maine. I was also AWOL, absent without leave from the Air Force. I had stolen some money from the motel owner where I was working. I suspected the police had been informed and were already looking for me. But they were probably unaware I was AWOL from the military.

I had not worn my uniform since going AWOL and was now wearing my Air Force blues. I hoped the uniform would increase my chances of getting away. As I sat on the bus, waiting, I thought, *Driver, please hurry; I need to get out of this town.*

When I was much younger, I lived in an orphanage where I often avoided getting caught for misbehaving. This time, I was hoping to elude the police. Finally, the bus was moving; each mile further on added to my confidence of getting away. After only a few miles the bus stopped. A policeman came onto the bus. He announced, '*I need to see everyone's identification.*'

Jack McCabe

Canada was only a few miles north, so I hoped he was just looking for people coming into the USA illegally. I took out my military identification card and held it up. The officer continued up the aisle, studying each passenger's papers. When he came by my seat, he barely glanced at me or my ID and moved toward the rear of the bus. Moments later he turned and came back toward the front. He stopped at my seat, and said, *'Let me see your ID again.'* Feeling very nervous, I handed him my military ID. He studied it and suddenly looked down at me and directed, *'Come with me off the bus.'*

As I got out of my seat, I reached up to retrieve my duffel bag, located on the rack above. Suddenly, my right arm was twisted behind my back. He was holding my arm with his right hand. His left hand was holding my shirt collar which felt extremely tight around my neck. The policeman was large, well over six feet and very strong. I was barely five foot six and weighed only a hundred and thirty-five pounds. He quickly pushed me down the steps and out the door, and slammed me against the side of the bus. My hands were behind my back, something metallic holding them together. I was overcome with fear, afraid to even move. Suddenly I realized I had pissed in my pants. I felt the officer's hands searching me. He removed my wallet. *'Do you have a gun?'* he demanded.

I was consumed with fear and had lost control of my voice. *'Answer me!'* he yelled. I mumbled, *'In my duffle bag.'*

'Stay put!' he ordered. I saw the bus driver bringing my

duffle bag, handing it to the policeman. I thought, *Oh, God! I'm caught! This is not supposed to be happening. How did I get into this trouble?*

I was in the back seat of a police car with my hands cuffed. I started to think. *What had I been doing before I got myself into this terrible situation? Yesterday I was walking around, feeling free and safe.*

Several months earlier I had gone AWOL from an airbase in Texas. I hitchhiked across the country, eventually arriving in Calais (pronounced "callous"). It was a small town in Maine on the border with Canada. I arrived there two weeks ago, broke and in need of a job. An employment agent sent me to a motel. They needed someone to help clean and make beds in their guest cabins. The motel owner, Mr. Robinson, was a friendly, older man. He hired me and gave me a place to sleep as well as daily meals. I had been working there two weeks, when one day, Robinson told me he was going into town and would be back in an hour or so.

When he left, I went into his house, found his bedroom, and explored some of his clothes drawers. I saw the money, a stack of bills, wrapped with a rubber band: mostly fives, tens, and twenties.

Without thinking I put the money in my pocket and decided to hightail it out of the area. I hustled to my bedroom, packed my duffle bag and tossed in the small pistol I had recently purchased. While swiftly walking to town I thought, *I need to get away, but how? Tomorrow, there's a bus going south.*

Jack McCabe

For tonight, I'll get a room in the hotel next to the bus station in Calais.

The next morning in my hotel room, I put on my blue Air Force uniform and then went to the bus station and bought a ticket to Boston. I sat on the bus, anxiously waiting for the vehicle to start moving. It did, but then the police found me and I was caught.

Sitting in the police car, I saw the bus leaving. The policeman was in the driver's seat talking on his radio. A voice said, '*Take him to the jail in Calais.*' In Calais, the policeman took me to a one-story brick building. Another officer led me to the cellar. He locked me in a room with bars on the door. Inside, just below the ceiling was a window, also covered with bars. It looked out on a parking lot. In the cell was a metal cot with a mattress. I felt tired and lay down to sleep.

The next morning, I was in the back seat of another police car. A wire partition was between me and the officer who was driving the car. I asked him, '*Where are we going?*' He replied, '*Kid, you stole some money. You're headed for the county jail in Machias.*' I was worried and explained, '*They got all their money back, plus some of mine. When will they let me go?*' The officer replied, '*Kid, it's not that simple.*'

When we arrived at the jail in Machias another officer directed me to a room with a counter containing a stack of prison uniforms. He told me to put on a prison outfit and to place my military clothes in my duffle bag. Rummaging through the stack of prison clothes, I found a pair of blue pants with a stipe and a matching shirt that fit me. After stuffing my Air Force uniform into my duffle bag, I put on the prison clothes. The officer put my duffle bag behind the counter and told me my clothes would be returned upon my release from jail.

The officer told me he was the jailer, and would lock us prisoners in our cells at night. He led me downstairs to a door with bars. We entered a large room where I saw some stairs leading up to a walkway. There were eight jail cells below the stairs. Looking up, I saw that the walkway had a railing on one side and more cells on the other side.

Opposite the walkway was a large wall containing three small barred windows, each located too high for anyone to see out.

Although the jailer wore a police uniform, he didn't carry a gun. He led me up the stairs to the walkway, then to the open door of a cell located around the corner from the other cells. The jailer told me I would be the only prisoner in this area. I looked below and saw some prisoners sitting on benches, located on both sides of two long tables. They were looking up at me. The jailer noticed this and suggested, '*Try staying away from the other prisoners. Some are here for getting drunk in public and starting fights; some others broke into homes and stole things. Avoid getting involved with them. You only need to sit with them at meal time.*'

The jailer left, and I entered my cell. It looked to be about six feet wide by eight feet deep, and contained a narrow metal cot with a mattress. On the mattress sat a stack of clean bedding with a pillow on top. To the side of the cot were a sink and a commode attached to the back wall. A roll of toilet paper rested on the side of the sink, near the commode.

I put a pillowcase on the pillow and made the bed. I was bored and sat down on the cot, contemplating my situation. After a few minutes, the jailer brought me a magazine and two books. I supposed he was treating me kindly, because I was only seventeen, much younger than the other prisoners.

When lunch arrived, I exited my cell and went below. There were six men sitting at one of the tables; each was eating from a tray of food. Their table appeared to be full. Two men sat at the other table, eating from their trays of food. Two other men stood nearby, talking. I saw three more trays of food on this table. I picked up one and sat down, leaving as much space as possible between me and the two men already sitting there. A few moments later, the two men who had been standing, each picked up one of the remaining trays and sat, one on my left, the other on my right. I felt small and intimidated. As I started to eat, the man on my left looked at me and asked, '*What are you in for?*'

All the prisoners were looking at me. I tried to avoid making eye contact with any of them, but felt I needed to acknowledge the question. I quietly answered, '*I stole some money.*' More questions were asked, and I kept my answers brief and vague.

When lunch was over and the tables were cleaned, I started

Ominous Beginnings

to go back up to my cell. One of the younger men came to me and invited me to join him and two others in a card game. The man seemed friendly, and I was feeling lonely, so I agreed to join them. The game was called rummy. As we four played and talked, I began to feel more comfortable. They seemed to accept me as one of the guys.

We played for a while then suddenly, we heard two men yelling at each other. The sounds came from the communal bathroom where toilets and showers were located. We stopped playing cards and went to see what was going on. The two men had started to fight. Some prisoners were shouting, urging one fighter to hit the other. The jailer and another officer rushed in, separated the fighters and locked them in their cells. We four card players returned to our game of rummy. The jail became relatively quiet again.

Most days there were about twelve prisoners in the jail. We got three meals each day, but with little variety: scrambled eggs and toast for breakfast, a ham and cheese sandwich at lunch, bread with either chicken noodle soup or beef stew and rice for supper. Water was available from the sink in our cells.

On Sundays, the routine in the jail was broken by a visit from a man and a woman. They came in carrying Bibles and hymnbooks, and offered to hold a church service. Some men participated, but I always declined. In the orphanage, I had grown tired of listening to those songs and hearing those same warnings and promises preached at me.

The jailhouse was located in Machias, Maine, the very

town I had been born in, seventeen years earlier. One day, the jailer came to me and said, '*You have a visitor.*' He led me to the room where visitors meet with prisoners. I entered and saw my brother. Gordon, now thirty-two, was fourteen years older than I was. He went by the name of Buster and had visited me twice when I lived in the orphanage. During the summer when I was thirteen, I lived with Buster for two weeks. I had forgotten I had a brother and wondered how he knew I was here in jail.

Meeting Buster, I felt embarrassed. He said, '*Hello Johnny. I wish we were meeting under better circumstances. I happened to be traveling in the area, visiting with our Aunt Barbara. She read about you in the local paper. I wish I could help you, but right now I really can't.*'

Buster didn't ask me why I stole the money, and I didn't tell him I was AWOL. He didn't question me and seemed to understand I had accepted the consequences of my actions. We talked about our family for a while. He expressed concern for me and made me an offer, '*Johnny, when you get out of this situation, come and see me. I will help you.*'

As Buster was leaving, I thanked him for visiting. On his way out, he stopped and turned toward me and said, '*Johnny, did you know our Grandfather McCabe was once the sheriff of this county? He was in charge of this jail.*'

After Buster's visit ended, I forgot all about him. I was in jail and was worried about what was going to happen to me. One day, a man dressed in a suit and tie visited me in the jail. He told me he had been assigned to advise me and to accompany me when I went before the judge. He explained the police had found a large sum of money in my wallet, and they believed I stole it from the motel. They had charged me with a serious crime, a felony. The man explained, '*People convicted of a felony can be put in jail for several years.*'

He then said, '*Luckily you are still a teenager. The worst that can happen is you can be sent to a reform school. If that happens, you will remain there until you turn twenty-one.*' The lawyer had already met with the judge, who had agreed to sentence me to one-year probation and release me to the Air Force, but only if I pled guilty. Before the man left, he told me I was scheduled to go before the judge the following week and advised, '*When we go to court, you should plead guilty.*'

I was dressed in my Air Force blues as the jailer escorted me into a courtroom, located in a building next to the jailhouse. There, I met my lawyer. We entered a courtroom and sat up front in chairs behind a desk facing a long and tall bench. Behind us were rows of benches like in a church. My lawyer told me to look at the people behind us. I turned and saw two Air Force military policemen (MPs) in uniform, sitting two rows back. My lawyer told me that the military police were there, waiting to take me back to the Air Force. He then asked, '*Are you ready to plead guilty?*' I said, '*Yes.*'

The judge came in, and I heard someone say, '*All rise.*' Everyone in the courtroom stood. The judge said something, and we all sat down. There was some lawyer talk, and then my lawyer told me to stand.

When I stood, the judge looked directly at me and asked, '*Son, how do you plead?*' I responded, '*Guilty, your Honor.*'

The judge said, '*John McCabe, I sentence you to one-year probation.*' He then added, '*The prisoner is now remanded to the Air Force.*'

I turned to my lawyer, thanked him, telling him good-bye. The two MPs came forward and handcuffed me. As we left the courtroom, one MP was carrying my duffle bag.

The MPs drove me to Dow Air Force Base, located near Bangor, Maine. I was put in the stockade. My days were spent marching and picking up trash all over the base, together with a few other incarcerated recruits.

Several weeks later, two Air Force MPs accompanied me by train to Amarillo, Texas, and then to the military air base from where I had gone AWOL. I was in the stockade there when a military court found me guilty of going AWOL. They punished me with an Undesirable Discharge along with two more months behind bars.

Early Orphanage Life

'Life is ten percent what happens to you and ninety percent how you respond to it.' —Lou Holtz

The year before I was born, my father, Gordon, and my mother, Carolyn, lived with their five children in Machias, Maine, the seat of Washington County. When I was born on December 5, 1935, my siblings included Helene (sixteen), Gordon Junior (fourteen), Margaret (twelve), Joan (four), and Jean (three).

Gordon McCabe Sr. atop the Rock of Gibraltar

Jack McCabe

My father had served as a merchant marine during the First World War. He returned home to marry Carolyn, who was a math teacher at the Machias Academy. He went into business, owning a movie house and a pool hall in Machias.

At the age of forty, my father began suffering from diabetes. His mother-in-law, Esther Leighton, had moved to Florida some years earlier and was concerned about Gordon's health, and the welfare of her daughter, Carolyn. Grandmother Leighton made Gordon an offer. If he would move our family to Florida, she would help Carolyn raise the children. In 1936, our family moved to Auburndale, a small town in central Florida where Granny Leighton was living.

The McCabe Family, circa 1935
Gordon Sr, Gordon Jr, Helene, Margaret, Joan, Jean

During the family's first year in Florida, Carolyn became pregnant. I was not yet two. She already had six children and must have dreaded raising another. One day, while my father was away visiting his doctor, my mother attempted to abort the unborn baby. When my father came home, he found his wife bleeding profusely. My mother died before anyone could save her.

Carolyn Leighton McCabe

Two years later, my father's health declined further. He lost a leg and used a wheelchair to get around. In 1939, he was placed in a veteran's hospital in Tampa, some forty miles from our home in Auburndale. He eventually lost his other leg. Granny Leighton, a widow, was suddenly responsible for four of her six grandchildren.

My oldest sister Helene was already twenty, married and living in Miami with her husband, Richard Hawkins. Gordon Jr, now eighteen, joined the Civilian Conservation Corps (known as the CCC). This New Deal program was started by President Roosevelt during the Great Depression.

Jack McCabe

Margaret (sixteen), Joan (seven), Jean (six), and I (four) were living at home with Granny. Margaret, now called Peggy, stayed home for another year before being sent off to "finishing school," a boarding school in Georgia.

Granny desired for us youngest three to be raised together, in a Christian environment. In February 1940, she placed us in Thornwell Orphanage. The institution was a Presbyterian Church supported home and school for children, located 350 miles north, in Clinton, South Carolina. My first residence at Thornwell was the Baby Cottage.

During my eleven years at Thornwell, I also stayed in other cottages: The Fowler, the Georgia-Beatie, the Hollingsworth and the McCormick. Mr. and Mrs. Cyrus McCormick provided the money to build this latter cottage. They also funded the construction of two other cottages named Edith and Harriet, after their daughters. All three cottages were architecturally the same.

Other cottage names were: Anita, Augustine, Fairchild, Faith, Florida, Silliman and Virginia. These residences were all built of stone from quarries in Laurens County, where the town of Clinton was located. They all had beautiful wood interiors and were built to last decades.

Each cottage had communal bathrooms, bedrooms and staircases made of hardwood. They each had a large porch, and there was a fireplace on each floor. Bedrooms on the upper floors had fire-escape ropes attached to the wall, near the windows. Each stood on more than an acre of land, providing significant playground space.

The campus also included two school buildings, an infirmary, a church, a dining facility and various maintenance facilities. Except for the Baby Cottage, each residence housed a single gender group of kids in the same age range. The fifty-acre campus was located on the west side of South Broad Street, just two blocks from the center of Clinton. An entry road off Broad gave access to the center of the campus. Upon entering, one saw a large church on the left and Faith Cottage on the right.

The Home of Peace was further north of Faith. Memorial Hall, a large dining facility, was located a little south and east of the Home of Peace. The entry road led straight to the main office. A maintenance facility was just north of the office, with a road between them that led west to Thornwell Street. The campus was bound on the north by Centennial Street. Thornwell Street ran through the campus, beginning at Centennial and ending at West Calhoun Street, the south boundary of the campus. Further west was a dirt road running north of West Calhoun, ending at the Silliman Cottage.

Some three hundred children were residing at Thornwell. My first memories are from the time I lived at the Baby Cottage. It was located on the corner of South Broad and West Calhoun. The campus of Presbyterian College began a block further south on Broad. I was one of some fifteen children, all younger than seven, residing in the cottage. We ate together, played on the swings in the backyard and took baths in metal tubs. We attended kindergarten in the front room.

My Kindergarten Class

One day, a woman came to the Baby Cottage and told me my father died. I was four, with no memory of my father. I felt nothing regarding his death. I had no memory of my mother, my grandmother, or any of my family. I was not even aware that Jean and Joan were residing there in another cottage.

I remember an older girl reading from a colorful story book. It was about a family: a father and mother with two young children, a boy and a girl. They all seemed so happy. Pictures in the book made me want to be part of a family. I was five at the time and wanted to be like the boy in the pictures.

Sometimes I would hear trains passing through town. Their whistles, as well as the sounds of drums and music coming from the college, caused me to wonder. '*What would*

Early Orphanage Life

it be like to live someplace else?

I heard the word "war" and a strange word, "Japanese," the name of people living far away. Japan had attacked Pearl Harbor on December 7, 1941, "a Day of Infamy." This historical event occurred two days after I turned six.

Johnny, Age 5

When I was six, I moved from the Baby Cottage to the Fowler Cottage. It was located on the east side of Thornwell Street, near the corner of Centennial, across the road from the Mary Jacobs Academy, the elementary school.

Miss Barker was the Fowler Cottage house matron, an older unmarried lady in charge of us. She marched us to the dining hall where we ate our meals. All, except those living in the Baby Cottage, went to this large facility for their meals. As we marched, Miss Barker was always telling the older boys to take their hands out of their pockets. I was too young to understand her concern.

The dining facility was a two-story building with a kitchen on the first floor and a large dining hall on the second. Some adults and a few orphan girls prepared our meals. Breakfast was either oatmeal or eggs and grits.

During the war years we didn't get much sugar, but we did get lots of molasses. Some of the food, such as milk, eggs and chicken, came from our farm. At Sunday lunch, we always had fried chicken, mashed potatoes, rolls and English peas. Sometimes we had dessert, usually rice pudding, but I had an ongoing desire for ice cream.

In the dining hall everyone sat at tables designated for their respective cottage. Kids, serving as waiters, brought large bowls of food from the kitchen and placed them on each table. The cottage house mothers served the food. We had three meals each day. At mealtimes, I would see my two youngest sisters.

I cannot recall when I first encountered my sisters, Jean and Joan. My memories of them are from when Jean was ten and Joan was eleven. I was about seven. I remember Joan as slight built, with light brown hair, a bookworm who displayed very little animation. She seemed disinterested in me. After Joan graduated and left Thornwell, she joined the US Army.

Early Orphanage Life

Joan Marie McCabe

Jean was also slight, with light brown hair. She was friendly and often gave me some attention. Jean and I became somewhat close. She learned to play the piano and eventually earned a music scholarship to Florida State University (an all-girls college at the time).

Jack McCabe

Jean Ruth McCabe

One night, when I was nine, the old high school building burned. It was located near the Baby Cottage. Suddenly, only four smoking walls stood where a three-story building was once located. The Fowler Cottage, where I was residing, was needed for classrooms, so it became the junior and senior high school. The Fowler kids were moved to the Georgia-Beatie Cottage.

Residing in each cottage was an older, unmarried woman, called a matron. She was in charge of the residence and its occupants. Most of us boys considered them the enemy. Each matron seemed to have her favorites, but I was never one of them.

When we misbehaved, they could spank us with a paddle or switch us with the branch of a bush. I was spanked several times, usually with my pants down. Both my sore bottom and I looked forward to the day we would escape the orphanage.

My new home, the Georgia-Beatie, was located on the north side of West Calhoun, just west of the Florida Cottage. Across the road from these cottages were large fields used for growing sorghum. This harvested crop was stored in a silo at the farm and was fed to the dairy cows.

Our playground was large and included over one hundred feet along West Calhoun and over two hundred feet along Thornwell Street. The front door of the Georgia-Beatie faced south, away from the main campus and was seldom used. Everyone entered through the back door, leading from our backyard into a large room. It was our indoor playground and study hall. Each of us had a cabinet there for storing our toys, schoolbooks, as well as paper and pencils. Study hall occurred every school night.

In the middle of the cottage was a hardwood staircase leading to the floors above. Most of us had bedrooms on the second floor where we shared a room with one other boy. A few double rooms on the third floor served other boys. Each floor had a bathroom down the hall, with toilets and a group shower.

Jack McCabe

Miss Janie Stewart, a tall, skinny, older woman, was the house matron. She was in charge of us. She had an apartment with a private bath on the second floor. Buck Shaw was my roommate. Our room was right next to her apartment. She felt the need to keep an eye on us. Buck and I were good friends, and we occasionally tested her patience (e.g., knock on her door late at night, slip a lit firecracker under her door).

Miss Stewart constantly found fault with my behavior. Sometimes, it was not what I did, but what I didn't do that displeased her. For example, if she asked me to pull weeds, I pretended to work for a short while, then, when she wasn't looking, I left and hid out in the bathroom. After finding me, Miss Stewart would treat me to one of her loud verbal admonishments. I didn't like being told what to do.

I often questioned her work assignments and tried not to let her reactions bother me. Weekdays, when we were not in school, Miss Stewart made us all work: weeding flower beds, raking yards, washing windows and scrubbing walls. We wanted time to play, but were only free for such after supper, and then, only if it was still light out and not raining.

On Saturday we could play after finishing our work assignments. On Sunday mornings we had to attend church. Then, in the afternoons, Miss Stewart made us take a nap. I was never sleepy and lay in my bed fantasizing about running away.

We were not allowed to leave the campus. There were no fences but we were all aware of the borders. Occasionally I would scale the invisible wall and walk along some streets nearby. I would pass by a home and see children playing in their yard. I wanted to meet them, but they just stared at me then looked away. They probably figured I was from the nearby orphanage and had been told to avoid us kids.

I didn't like being an orphan. I desired to live in a real home. I wanted to choose when to play and what to eat. I often thought of running away. One day I did take off but got lost in the woods. After an hour or so I found my way back. I told no one where I had been.

The Georgia-Beatie contained a room where our dirty clothes collected as we threw them down a laundry chute that led straight down from the second floor to the basement. To be considered a 'MAN,' you had to jump from the second floor and land on a pile of dirty clothes. I survived the fall many times.

The ages of boys residing at the Georgia-Beatie ranged from eight to twelve. Several of us had been together since first arriving at the Baby Cottage. There was a jungle gym outside in the yard, a structure made of horizontal and vertical bars, on which we enjoyed climbing. As we got older, softball became our main outdoor activity.

Sometimes, two of us would get into a fight, usually ending rather quickly. It was during these fights we established our individual level of toughness. I won some fights, but lost most. I didn't like to fight, and when confronted by a kid who was tougher than I was, I would try to joke and talk my way out of it.

During one softball game, I swung my bat and connected with the ball. The bat slipped out of my hands and went flying toward third base where my buddy Wallace was standing. The bat hit Wallace. He became angry and came rushing toward me at first base.

He smacked my right ear with his fist. It stung like hell. I grabbed him and wrestled him to the ground while shouting, *'I'm sorry! I'm sorry! I didn't mean to hit you!'*

Wallace slowly calmed down, and I let him up without him saying, *'Uncle.'* We both let it go and the game continued. This incident was typical. For the most part, we all got along pretty well. Usually, no one held a grudge after the punches and wrestling stopped.

I had never met my brother and was essentially unaware of him. Earlier in the week, Miss Stewart said my brother would be visiting soon.

When I first saw him, he was wearing a military uniform. He shook my hand and smiled saying, *'Johnny, I'm your brother. My name is Gordon but my friends call me Buster. I just got out of the Army.'* I could see a bit of myself in his face. The shape of his mouth, nose and eyes were similar to mine. He was the first man to shake my hand, and I immediately felt comfortable with him.

Buster gave me an Army flashlight. It did not use batteries. To power it, one needed to repeatedly squeeze the grip. No other kid had a flashlight like that, so I felt special. I showed

Early Orphanage Life

him my bicycle and he asked, '*Where did you get the bike?*'

I explained, '*Some of us have sponsors who send money and gifts to the orphanage. My sponsor sent me the bicycle as a Christmas present. The first time I rode it, I ran head on into a pine tree. I was looking at my feet instead of where I was going.*' We both laughed.

Gordon C. McCabe Jr.

I asked him what it was like in the Army. Buster explained. He had enlisted in the US Army a few months before the end of World War II. After he had completed basic training, the Army had sent him to school to learn how to repair radios. The war ended soon after he completed his radio repair training, so he was given an early discharge.

Buster told me he was currently attending college at Temple University in Philadelphia. We talked more, and I told Buster, '*I wish I had a basket on my bike so I could carry things.*' He responded, '*Let's talk about that tomorrow.*' Buster then left for his hotel.

He returned the next day, and we talked about finding a bike shop. I told him, '*There's one down Broad Street, near the town square.*' I felt excited as we walked the bike together, off the campus. When we got to the bike shop, we saw several baskets in stock. Buster helped me choose one. He bought it for me, then borrowed some tools from the shop owner and attached the basket.

Returning to the campus, Buster walked while I rode my bike. I circled him, and thanked him for the basket, and told him how happy I felt. Later that afternoon, Buster said his good-byes. He had to leave, and I felt sad to see him go. But I was proud that I now had a big brother.

There was a large swimming pool with diving boards located behind the Fowler school house. Holding the edge of the pool in the deep end, I would let go and dogpaddle. After a minute or two, I would grab hold of the edge to feel safe. Eventually I was able to venture farther from the edge and dogpaddle for longer periods of time. In this manner, I taught myself to swim.

One day a young girl almost drowned in the pool. She was pulled out of the water and laid on her back, not moving, surrounded by a group of people. A big kid, the lifeguard, was pushing down on her, making water spew out of her mouth. The girl soon coughed, and the lifeguard helped her sit up. She was okay, and all the people cheered and clapped their hands. I felt detached from the crowd and the incident, but wondered, *what will death feel like?*

Every Sunday morning, we had to attend Sunday School, held in rooms at the back of the church. We repeatedly read the first and second Presbyterian Catechisms and were expected to memorize them. The main service began after Sunday school. Dr. MacDonald, the president of Thornwell, preached what seemed like a long sermon.

I learned about Jesus and heard that he had died for my sins, even the ones I had not yet committed. Again, and again, I heard, '*Let your conscience be your guide.*' I usually ignored mine.

Believing in God was easy, but I found it difficult to accept the stories and promises of Jesus. I sensed a discrepancy between mankind's ability to think and come to logical conclusions versus people accepting truths based on faith.

The dining hall was often the center of campus activity. It served as our auditorium. Each morning after breakfast, Dr. MacDonald stood on the raised stage at the far end of the dining hall and began the day with a prayer and a short sermon.

Some Saturday evenings the hall became a movie theater. A large screen would be placed on the stage. A movie would be shown on the screen. I recall viewing *How Green is my Valley* and *White Christmas*.

Jack McCabe

During my time at the Georgia-Beatie Cottage, Miss Stewart marched us to the dining facility three times every day. I once accidentally caused her a painful injury. It happened one evening when she was marching us to the dining hall for supper. Because I was one of the "bad" kids, I had to march in the rear with her. We were not supposed to talk.

I was whispering something to Billy, another "bad" boy. Miss Stewart swung at me with her purse, but I stepped out of the way. She tripped and fell, injuring one of her knees. For a while she was unable to walk without help and stayed at the Lesh infirmary. Even though my actions contributed to Miss Stewart's injuries, I considered the incident her fault and felt no guilt.

My favorite school subject was music. Our music teacher was Miss Luva McDonald. She played the piano and taught us to sing. Sometimes she had us listening to classical music: *Peter and the Wolf,* the *1812 Overture,* and the theme of the Lone Ranger radio program, *William Tell Overture.* The only other time I heard classical music was while watching *Tom and Jerry* and *Woody Woodpecker* in cartoons at the downtown movie theater.

My favorite teacher was Miss Boland who taught math. She told me I was smart and sometimes asked me to help other kids who had trouble learning math. Miss Boland told me I should become a math teacher when I grow up. I think today she would be proud of me because I taught math for almost fifty years.

Early Orphanage Life

When kids had their tonsils removed, or caught the mumps or measles, or got sick, they stayed in a bedroom at the Lesh Infirmary. It was a three-story building with a kitchen and offices on the first floor. Hospital rooms and bathrooms were on the floors above. A dumbwaiter type elevator was used to haul food from the kitchen to the floors above. This dumbwaiter was a box-like container, raised and lowered by ropes dangling in the elevator shaft. I once got caught riding in that contraption.

Billy and I were both eight and staying together in a room on the third floor. One night I was inside the dumbwaiter and Billy was hauling me up and down, giving me a ride. I couldn't reach the ropes, so Billy had to do all the pulling. It was late at night, and we thought the nurse was busy on the floors below.

She surprised Billy, and I heard her ask, '*Billy. What are you doing outside of your bedroom?*' He replied, '*Nothing.*'

The nurse then asked, '*Are you playing with the elevator? Is there someone in there?*' I heard Billy say, '*No.*'

I then heard the nurse say, '*Billy, stop fooling around and go back to your room.*' I was stuck in the dumbwaiter and heard her walking away. The nurse knew some kid was in the elevator, but left me trapped there for a while.

After what seemed a long time, the dumbwaiter descended to the kitchen. When the nurse opened it, she saw me and acted surprised. As I was getting out, the nurse said, '*Johnny McCabe, I hope you enjoyed your little adventure tonight. Next time I will leave you in there all night.*' The nurse acted like she was angry, but I had the feeling she actually approved of my adventure.

I once learned an important lesson while staying in the Lesh Infirmary. There were four of us boys in the same room. We were young, about seven. During supper one night we had used our spoons to flip mashed potatoes up on the ceiling where some of them stayed.

The next morning before breakfast, a nurse came in and asked each of us the same strange question, '*Did you have a bowel movement?*'

None of us knew what a "bowel" was, or how they moved. Was it about the potatoes still stuck up on the ceiling? We all felt guilty, so we each gave the same answer, '*No.*'

The nurse soon returned, rolling a tray containing glasses of some pink liquid, what looked to us to be milkshakes. They were not milkshakes. They were milk of magnesia. '*Yuck!*' After that incident I learned to say, '*Yes.*' when asked questions about bowel movements.

Early Orphanage Life

Johnny, Age 7

Becoming a Teenager

'Freedom is what you do with what's been done to you.' —Jean-Paul Sartre

When children at Thornwell turned twelve they were given duties. Boys either spent time cutting grass and raking leaves around the campus, or they worked on the farm.

A few lucky boys got to work in the print shop. At twelve, I moved to the Hollingsworth Cottage adjacent to the dairy. The ages of the boys residing there ranged from twelve to eighteen.

My first assignment was the chicken farm. Every morning, Wallace and I got up before 6:00 a.m. to feed hundreds of chickens. We collected dozens of eggs and delivered them to the dining hall kitchen. On Saturdays, Wallace and I prepared the fryers for Sunday dinner, a somewhat undesirable task.

After placing a chicken in an inverted metal cone-shaped container, I pulled its head out of the bottom of the cone and cut it off. The chicken's blood fell to a trough below where water flushed it down a drain. Holding the headless chicken by its legs, I dumped it into a tub of scalding hot water. Then I held it against rubber stubs sticking out of a rotating wheel which removed the chicken's feathers. Wallace cut the chicken open and removed its innards. Initially, I felt squeamish doing this work, but eventually got used to it.

In the heat of summer, we shoveled sawdust mixed with chicken manure into a spreader, another foul-smelling and unpleasant task. The mixture was used as fertilizer. Work on the chicken farm was considered the worst assignment.

The next year, Wallace and I were assigned to work at the dairy, helping some ten other kids. Except for removing cow manure from the barn where the milking took place, it was a much cleaner and more pleasant form of work. We boys milked some thirty cows twice daily. A heating process was used to pasteurize the milk before it was cooled and delivered to the dining hall kitchen.

Mr. Wickham was responsible for running the farm. He was a white man and hired several black men to work with him. These men plowed the fields and harvested the crops. We assisted the black men in the fields. We loaded hay on wagons and into the tops of storage barns. Farm tractors were used to pull the wagons and other farming machinery.

Sometimes, Willie, one of the black men, let me drive the tractor. He also gave me driving lessons using the farm truck. Willie and the other black men were always kind and friendly. We joked around with them.

Thornwell had a large laundry building where several black women worked. It was hot inside the building, so its large glass windows were usually open. I looked in and saw women using some fascinating machines.

They washed sheets and towels in huge tubs and dried them in even larger machines. They fed a dry sheet into one end of a wide machine, and it traveled over and under lots of rollers and came out the other end completely ironed. If only I could put my troubles through machines like those.

When girls turned twelve, they were given an assignment: the kitchen, the dining hall, the laundry, the Baby Cottage, the Lesh Infirmary, or the sewing shop. Girls who worked at the sewing shop also sorted used clothing. On Saturdays, they could earn some money working at a rummage sale where these clothes were sold.

I often needed money to spend downtown for a soda or some ice cream. My sister Jean worked at the rummage sale and sometimes gave me part of her earnings. I also earned money by collecting empty soda bottles from around construction sites, returning them to the filling station for a penny each. But I had another way of getting money; a faster, though sinful way.

Sometimes I went to the chicken farm, put a couple of fryers in a feed sack and took them to Colored Town, where I sold them to black families. A few other kids also sold chickens. We knew it was wrong. Perhaps I should have asked Jesus to forgive me.

Two skilled carpenters worked in the tech building. They used powerful woodworking machines to cut and shape wood and to repair things made of wood. They were friendly and answered my questions about their work and their tools.

The tech building also had a print shop used to produce a monthly newspaper. The paper was mailed to churches and families who provided financial support for Thornwell. This print shop contained a Linotype and a printing machine.

Mr. Stutts used the Linotype to stamp words on blank pieces of lead. He placed these lead pieces in wooden racks and stacked the racks in the printing machine. When he fed blank pieces of paper into the printing machine they exited as printed pages.

The print shop had a separate room containing a special stove used to melt lead. The soft lead was shaped into blank pieces to be used again in the Linotype. I sometimes sneaked into this room, melted some lead, and used various special molds to create metal animals. It was fascinating and lots of fun.

Thornwell Orphanage was bordered on the east by Broad Street. This road ran north and south in the small town of Clinton, South Carolina. It was also state highway 72, running north from Greenwood to Clinton then turning east toward Whitmire. I often walked a few blocks north on this street to visit the gas station where I purchased candy and a soda. In those days gas stations were called filling stations. It was there I collected my first free road maps.

A soda fountain was located another block up on the right where I paid fifteen cents for a 'blizzard,' a large and delicious ice cream concoction. Further up on the left was the movie theater where I paid eleven cents to see a 'picture show.' The city also had other retail stores including a dry goods store named Belk. We young kids walked in a group to this store once a year, usually in the fall to buy a pair of shoes. Before turning twelve, we wore shoes only in the winter months.

Another highway passing through town was US 76. I often wondered about these highways. *Where did these roads go? Which highway led to Florida where I lived before coming to the orphanage?* The summer of 1948 brought me an opportunity to travel some of these roads.

My oldest sister, Helene, was living in Florida with her husband, Richard, and their two daughters, Carol (five), and Linda Gail (three). Helene and Richard invited Joan (seventeen), Jean (sixteen), and me (twelve) to stay with them during the summer of 1948. One day around noon, the three of us left Clinton by Greyhound and began our trip south.

During the night the bus was traveling through Georgia. Its lights reflected off highway signs. Bright billboards appeared in the distance. As the bus approached these reflections and billboards, I thought we were arriving in the next town. This sequence of false arrivals kept me awake. Views out the windows were constantly changing and they kept me anticipating the next town. I didn't dare go to sleep for fear of missing something new.

Just before dawn, the bus arrived in Jacksonville. We needed to change busses for the trip further south. After an hour or so, we boarded a different Greyhound. It was daylight, and I could see water as the bus crossed over rivers. During midmorning, this second bus stopped in Orlando (a small town in those days), picked up some passengers and continued on to Tampa. By the time we arrived at the bus station there, our trip had covered some 350 miles.

We were met by our oldest sister, Helene Hawkins and her husband, Richard. It had been eight years since Helene had last seen her three youngest siblings. She seemed happy to be meeting us again. She was twenty-eight, slender and pretty, with a friendly smile.

Richard barely remembered us, but he made us feel welcomed. He was thirty-two, slight, with black hair and dark eyes, and stood about five feet, seven inches. These two adults were to play an important role in my life.

Richard and Helene Hawkins

Becoming a Teenager

Richard drove Helene and us three kids to see our Grandmother Leighton. After sending us to Thornwell, she had visited us only once. Her visit occurred in the spring of 1946 when I was ten. I had expected my grandmother to be kind and friendly, but during that one visit, she seemed cold and distant.

In the summer of 1948, Granny lived in Tampa. Her apartment was located on Bayshore Boulevard, near the water and close to the center of the city. Tampa was an exotic and tropical city, with palm trees and other strange looking plants. Granny greeted us with very little warmth. I could sense no kindness in her responses to anything I said. Her disposition seemed consistent with the poorly chosen gift she had sent me for my tenth birthday.

Granny's package came in the shape of a box of candy and was delivered to the Georgia-Beatie Cottage with my name on it. The gift sat on a shelf out of my reach, not to be opened until my birthday, several days away. I was greatly disappointed when I opened the box. My grandmother had sent me a Bible. At that Christian orphanage, Bibles were more common than brooms.

Granny Leighton obviously had strong feelings regarding my religious upbringing. She had raised only a daughter and probably had no experience nurturing young boys. She later remembered me in her will, thoughtfully leaving me money I used while attending college. I eventually forgave her for sending me a disappointing birthday gift.

After our short visit with our grandmother in Tampa, Richard drove us to their home in Bartow. There I met my two nieces, Carol and Linda Gale. I was suddenly the only boy in a family with five children, getting lots of attention. I felt I could easily live with this family.

In 1939, after Richard and Helene were married, they had offered to take the three of us and raise us in their home. For some unknown reason, Granny Leighton never accepted their generous offer.

During my stay with them the summer of 1948, Helene and Richard made me feel appreciated. They seemed to accept me for who I was. Their kind attention delighted me. In the orphanage, I was seldom shown any affection, so this was a new and wonderful experience.

I wanted to remain with the Hawkins family, but when summer was over, we three kids boarded a bus for the return trip to Clinton. During the trip back, I daydreamed about visiting again next summer.

Hosting all three of us the summer of 1948 had been too much for the Hawkins family, so for the summer of 1949, only Jean was invited to visit. Joan had graduated and joined the Army, and I was supposed to wait and visit the following summer. I didn't want to wait.

I was thirteen and had heard about hitchhiking. I decided to try thumbing my way to Florida. Using those road maps from the filling station, I decided to start on US 76 and hitchhike toward Laurens and Anderson. Traveling in that direction led to Georgia. Other roads there led to Florida.

One day, right after lunch, with two dollars and some change in my pocket, I left the campus carrying some clothes in a small cardboard suitcase. I walked to the west side of town and stood on the side of the road. Each time a car approached I extended my arm with my thumb raised. Soon a car stopped and the driver, a man, asked, '*Where you going son?*'

'*Anderson,*' I said.

He responded, '*Jump in, kid. I'll get you as far as Greenville.*' The first ride was followed by many more. I rode in all kinds of cars and trucks, some with just a driver and some with families. Whenever a driver dropped me off, I walked to the other side of town and caught my next ride. My favorite rides were with truck drivers. They liked to talk and let me help them when they made a delivery.

That evening, I was on the southern outskirts of Macon, Georgia, heading south on US 23. It was about to get dark and I was tired, so I looked for a place to stay for the night. I saw a billboard up on a hill overlooking the highway. There were no lights shining on the large sign, so I decided to sleep underneath it. I used some clothes as a pillow and went to sleep.

Just before sunrise, I awoke with ants stinging me. After wiping them off, I put on my jacket. The early morning fog had brought a chill to the air. I had survived my first night on the road, and as a result, I felt elated and confident.

My third ride the next day was with two college boys from

Tennessee, heading for Florida. I listened to them talk about life at school and concluded college must be a nice place to live. One of the boys asked me if I was hungry and told me they planned to stop in Waycross for breakfast. I had already spent my money. After I explained I had no money, he said, '*Tell me about yourself, and I'll buy you breakfast.*'

I didn't want to tell him I was running away from an orphanage, so I made up a story. While we sat in the restaurant ordering our meals, I began telling my made-up story.

The boy who promised to buy me breakfast interrupted me and said, '*No, no. I want to hear the truth.*' I felt ashamed about lying and told them I was hitchhiking from South Carolina to visit my oldest sister in Florida. They both laughed and said they were glad to help me.

We continued our trip south from Waycross on US 1. That highway runs from somewhere in northern Maine all the way to Key West, Florida. In the early afternoon, we arrived in Daytona Beach where they were going to stay. As I was getting out of the car, each boy wished me good luck and handed me a dollar bill. I was surprised and pleased. Complete strangers could be kind and generous.

In Daytona, I walked for a while on a sandy beach and for the first time, saw the ocean. Looking at the distant horizon, I wondered if Africa was on the other side. After walking through town, I caught a ride on US 92 to Deland and then to Orange City. Years later, I had a twenty-year career in this part of Florida.

Becoming a Teenager

I continued hiking south to Lake Wales, then turned east on state highway 60, arriving in Bartow just before sundown. Helene and Richard were quite surprised at my arrival. But they both made me feel welcomed. They phoned the orphanage and informed them of my arrival. I was surprised that my escape had been so easy.

Richard was an insurance salesman. Most days he made short trips to visit his customers and other people. He collected monthly insurance payments from his clients and tried to sell insurance policies to others.

During my second visit, Richard often let me ride with him on his travels. When he stopped for business, I usually sat in the car or walked around within sight of the car. On those trips, we ate many lunches together and had interesting conversations. Richard was old enough to be my father and treated me like I supposed a dad treated a son. I admired him and was fond of him. I had the feeling he also liked me.

Helene and Richard's home, was located in central Florida, where citrus trees were common. There was a large grapefruit tree just outside their house and a grove of orange trees nearby.

Lunches often consisted of Helene's grilled cheese sandwiches and Royal Crown Colas from a nearby City Service gas station. My curiosity led me to explore the town of Bartow. I wanted to stay with the Hawkins family, but a Greyhound bus took Jean and me back to the orphanage.

Those first two ventures from the orphanage were not my last. I was to hit the road twice more. Each time I did, no one stopped or questioned me. I doubt the orphanage ever reported my absence to the police. I felt I was gaining some control over my life. I now had the means to escape the boredom and restlessness I felt while residing there.

Thornwell was coed, with about as many girls as boys. Until I was twelve, I spoke with girls only at school. As I grew older, I met and talked with them near their cottages, at athletic events and in the dining hall before and after meals. Some of them were friendly and liked to joke around. I enjoyed being with them and felt attracted to some of them.

In the spring of 1949, several of us seventh and eighth grade students were bused to a park on a lake near Greenwood. In the park, I noticed this particular seventh grade girl. A kid in her class had told me her name was Verna. I wanted to meet her, so I lingered near her. When I got close, I stared at her and when she looked my way, I smiled. She smiled back then turned away.

While the bus was loading for the return trip, I hung back and waited until I saw her get on the bus. As I boarded, I noticed the seat adjacent to her was empty, so I sat next to her and asked, '*Is your name Verna?*'

She looked up smiling and responded, '*Yes. How did you know?*' Her smile gave me confidence. Looking directly into her eyes, I replied, '*I asked some kid in your class.*' She smiled and I got a real pleasant feeling. I was immediately attracted to her.

As the bus rounded a corner, our shoulders touched, and

my left arm touched hers. I let my arm remain there then moved my hand to hers. On the way back to Thornwell, we held hands and made small talk. I felt very excited. It was a new feeling, and it seemed to promise something exciting.

I soon learned her name was Verna Kinion. She had also lost her parents. During the next school year, she turned thirteen and I turned fourteen. Each day, we met at school between and after classes.

Verna worked at the sewing shop, so I hung around outside until she got off work. When we were together, we talked and held hands. I wanted to be with her every waking moment.

The first time I kissed her, she kissed me back, and I felt a new and intensely pleasant sensation. Public displays of affection were not allowed, so our meetings had to be secret and private.

In the fall of 1950, I was fourteen and entered the ninth grade. I had moved to the McCormick Cottage. Inside the building was a large bathroom on the first floor with a coal-burning stove. The stove was used to heat water for the showers. During the winter, we got the water so hot only steam came out of the shower heads. We got wet and ran around outside in the freezing air to collect ice on our bodies. We then ran back and melted the ice in the steam. It was great fun.

That fall was when Buster visited me a second time. He told me he had graduated from college and was now an electrical engineer. He lived and worked in Philadelphia, a

Jack McCabe

large city in Pennsylvania. Soon after we met, Buster asked me if I still had my bicycle. I said, '*Yes*' and took him to see it. I wanted to show him the basket was still attached.

He studied my bike and decided it needed a new chain. We went to the bike shop where a technician installed a new one.

On our way back to the campus, we passed by a pawn shop. I was familiar with this store and asked Buster if we could go inside. He said, '*Yes.*' We entered and looked at all the stuff they sold there: hand guns under the glass counter, several rifles hanging on the wall behind the cash register and various musical instruments.

I often dreamed of owning a rifle; one like the cowboys use in the movies. I told Buster I would really like to have a rifle so I could go squirrel hunting with the other boys. He seemed surprised and asked me if I was allowed to have a rifle. I lied and told him, *'Yes, provided it's only a twenty-two.'*

I suspected Buster felt sorry for me because I lived in an orphanage, a place where he never had to stay. He bought me a twenty-two rifle and a box of bullets. A month later, I got into trouble with the rifle.

My room was on the third floor of the McCormick. There were lots of squirrels on our campus and many of them lived in a tree just outside my window. Those creatures had never heard the sound of a gun.

One day I poked my .22 rifle out my window and shot about twenty of them. The rifle was the one my brother had recently bought me. The squirrels all fell to the base of the same tree. Some boys quickly noticed the pile of dead squirrels. They determined I was the shooter and told the house matron. She informed Dr. MacDonald. He came to McCormick, took my rifle and gathered a bunch of kids to bear witness to my punishment.

MacDonald made me load the dead squirrels into a wheelbarrow, and then push the load to the farm. I had to dig a hole for each squirrel and bury them individually. MacDonald intended to embarrass me in front of the small crowd, but they just seemed amused by the whole affair. MacDonald never returned my rifle.

In the summer of 1951, I was fifteen and wanted to visit my brother, Buster. He was now twenty-nine and worked somewhere near Philadelphia. I left the campus and hitchhiked north with the intention of locating him. I traveled first to Columbia, South Carolina via US 76, planning to find my way to US 1. Columbia was a big city, and my maps did not show city streets. I had to stop and ask for directions. The first day, I walked a lot and slept that night in a shed located behind a church.

The next morning, I found US 1, walked north to a truck stop and bought breakfast. After eating, I met some truck drivers and asked them for a ride north. A driver hauling furniture toward Washington, DC, agreed to let me ride with him. On the way north he made several deliveries, and I helped him unload. His last delivery was in DC, where he told me the rest of the way to Philadelphia was mostly through cities. He then asked, '*Do you have money for a bus?*'

I responded, '*Nope.*'

He bought me a soda and a sandwich and gave me bus fare; another generous stranger.

In DC, I found my way to the bus station and learned the next bus to Philadelphia was scheduled to leave at seven in the morning. I walked several blocks outside the station and saw important looking buildings and several historical monuments. It was not yet dark, so I decided to spend time sightseeing.

I walked to the Capitol Building, then the entire length of the National Mall to the Washington Monument. After visiting the Lincoln Memorial, I walked along the Potomac River. When I reached a bridge crossing the river, the sun had gone down, so I turned back toward the city. As I walked by the White House, it was all lit up. All of Washington, DC, was ablaze with light. The city seemed like a fascinating and exciting place to live.

I spent the remainder of the night sleeping in the bus station located near Union Station. Once during the night, a policeman woke me up and asked me if I had a bus ticket. I showed him mine, and he left. The next morning, I boarded a Greyhound bus, arriving in Philadelphia around eleven.

I didn't know where Buster worked, lived, or how to reach him. I knew travelers who needed assistance could get help at train stations, so I walked into the thirtieth street railroad terminal. There, I saw a sign near a desk reading Travelers Aid and sought help from two ladies working behind the desk. They asked me lots of questions about my brother. I didn't know much about him, but I did know he had been in the US Army and had attended Temple University. One lady said, *'Wait here in the station and we will try to locate him.'*

I wandered around the station for hours while they attempted to find Buster. It was mid-afternoon when they told me they had located him. He would meet me at the station when he got off work.

When Buster met me, he told me he had been informed about my absence from Thornwell. The orphanage had called Helene and she had called him. He was surprised I had hitchhiked all the way to Philadelphia, but pleased I had arrived safely.

We rode on a trolley to his house in South Philly where he was staying with an older unmarried policeman, Pop Taylor. I had supper with them after which they showed me to a small room where I would be sleeping.

Buster and Pop Taylor left each morning for work. I was expected to stay close by the house. I explored some of the neighborhood, but spent most of my time either in the house, watching a small black and white television or on the front porch, watching the traffic drive by. The house was next to a trolley barn, and I was fascinated by those noisy vehicles. They were attached to overhead wires and rode on railroad tracks.

One day, Buster asked me if I had ever met my sister Peggy. I said, *'No.'* He told me she lived in New York and wanted us to visit. The following weekend he drove us to her house on Long Island, New York. Peggy lived in Uniondale, a Levittown village. This large tract of houses built after World War II, provided low-cost housing for returning servicemen and their families.

The houses all looked alike. Each was a boxlike, three-bedroom, one bath abode, with the same looking front entry and no garage. House numbers were the only clue for finding an address.

Peggy lived with her husband, Paul Boyajian, and their two small children, Paul Junior (two) and Caroline (four). Paul was about five foot nine, with black hair and was a little older than Buster. He was handsome with a friendly smile.

During World War II, Paul was in the Army Air Corps, stationed in Florida where he met Peggy. After he had been discharged, they married and moved north to New York. Peggy was now twenty-six, petite with brown hair. I thought she was pretty.

Our visit was short; only three hours. I was happy to meet Peggy's family and later spent some time living with them. Buster drove us back to Philly and several days later returned me to Thornwell by bus. Once again, I had escaped from the orphanage with no negative consequences.

In the fall of 1951, Verna, my first girlfriend, was fourteen and in the ninth grade. I was fifteen and in the tenth grade. We began to meet often, and our attraction to each other became intense. The adults at Thornwell knew that Verna and I had become an "item." They kept a close eye on us, but we found time and hiding places for our secret meetings. At school, we planned our next rendezvous. Some afternoons, we met in the church; its various rooms provided us privacy. The church became our personal sanctuary.

Verna Kinion, Age 14

Verna resided at the Fairchild Cottage, a couple of hundred yards from the McCormick where I was living. At midnight, I opened my third-floor window and dropped the fire-escape rope. After wrapping a towel around my hands, I slid down the rope to the porch roof below. The towel prevented the rope from burning my hands. A year earlier, on my first trip down a fire escape rope, I had badly burned my hands.

Once on the roof, I slid down a pole to the porch floor and made my way to the dirt road running behind Fairchild. There were no light poles near the Fairchild, so the road was dark. Arriving at her cottage, I signaled her with my flashlight. She came out the back door, barefoot, moving as quietly as a mouse. Together, we ran across the road to a garage where the farm truck was parked. Sitting in the cab of the truck, we talked and kissed and held each other. After an hour or so, we returned to our residences. I thought, *My life can never be better than it is during our nightly meetings.*

During the fall of 1951, Verna and I met almost every evening. One night, I jogged on the dirt road to the back of Fairchild. Verna came out the door, and we hustled to the garage and got into the farm truck. After an hour or so, we said our farewells and Verna ran back toward Fairchild. Suddenly, a police car turned off Thornwell Street and entered the dirt road, driving to the rear of Verna's cottage. It stopped and a spotlight came on, shining in the direction where Verna had stopped. She had seen the car and was hiding behind a pine tree.

I figured the policeman had seen her, so I stood in the middle of the road, intending to distract him. When he got out of his car, I hollered '*Hey!*' Seeing me, he got back in his car and started driving toward me.

I ran down the dirt road, away from where Verna was

hiding. Before the police car got close, I cut across to the back of the Virginia Cottage and quickly entered the back door. I stood just inside and watched. The patrol car stopped and the spotlight was directed toward the back of the Virginia. After a short time, the police car moved on.

I waited a while longer before returning to the McCormick. Back in my room, I retrieved the fire-escape rope. I had enjoyed another night of adventure with Verna. We had survived a close call; or so I thought.

Sketch of McCormick Cottage

The next day, the police reported the incident to the Thornwell authorities. The girls at the Fairchild Cottage were questioned, and one of them said she saw Verna enter from outdoors. Asking more questions, the house matron discovered Verna had been meeting with a boy. Verna and I had agreed, if we ever got caught, we would not reveal each other's identity. Dr. MacDonald, the president of Thornwell, was informed about Verna's behavior.

MacDonald quickly determined I was the boy and sent for me. After the squirrel incident, this was my second time getting into serious trouble. I wanted to avoid any confrontation, and took to the road, hitchhiking north, hoping to stay a while with my brother Buster.

It was late in the afternoon as I hitchhiked north. There were few cars on the road. Sometimes I had to wait hours between rides. I became discouraged and spent the night sleeping inside a barn located near the highway.

The next morning, I made it to Charlotte, North Carolina. After arriving there, I decided to call Buster and ask him if I could visit. Buster was not surprised; once again he had been informed of my absence from Thornwell. He told me to find the Western Union office where he would wire me bus fare. After collecting the money, I purchased a ticket to Philadelphia.

Buster no longer lived in Philly. He now lived thirty miles away, in Lancaster, and worked there as an engineer for a radio station. After getting off work, he drove to Philly and picked me up. Buster was residing alone in a rooming house in Lancaster. He got me a room in the same house.

Buster treated me with kindness. The first day, as he left for work, he gave me a few dollars and told me he trusted me to spend it wisely, and to stay out of trouble. I was not about to let my brother down.

I spent my days exploring the Lancaster area and going to movies where I ate lots of popcorn. I wanted to continue living with Buster, but after two weeks, he put me on a bus back to Thornwell.

It was late December 1951, when I arrived back at Thornwell. While I was away, Dr. MacDonald had contacted Helene, my sister in Florida, and asked her to take me off their hands. She had agreed, and I was soon "shipped out" on a bus, on my way south. I had just turned sixteen and was receiving my first "undesirable discharge." And I was finally escaping the orphanage.

Johnny, Age 16

A Road Trip

'Life is a lively process of becoming.'—
Douglas MacArthur

In 1940, when Joan, Jean and I were placed in the orphanage, Helene and Richard were married and living in Miami. Their first daughter, Carol, was born the same year. Later, Richard moved his family to Mulberry, Florida, where, in 1943, Linda Gail was born. World War II broke out in late 1941. Richard enlisted in the US

Army on June 29, 1944, and traveled by ship to Europe, arriving on December 18. He saw combat in the historic Battle of the Bulge, the last offensive effort of the Nazi army. After the war ended, he returned by ship to the USA, arriving on January 29, 1946, and was discharged on February 4, 1946. He was soon with his family in Mulberry again.

Sergeant Richard Hawkins

Bartow, the seat of Polk County was a small community located a few miles east of Mulberry and south of Lakeland. Mulberry was the phosphate mining capitol of the world; Lakeland was the citrus growing center of Florida. These towns are located in central Florida.

In 1952, I was sixteen and arrived in Mulberry, Florida, to join the Hawkins family. Earlier, Thornwell Orphanage had decided my behavior was inconsistent with the expectations they had for children in their care. Helene and her husband, Richard, had agreed to take me off their hands.

A Road Trip

Helene Hawkins

Richard was the manager of a grocery store, owned by a local family and located in Mulberry. Helene worked in the office of Badcock Industries, a company with several furniture stores throughout Florida. Badcock was also owned by a local Mulberry family. My nieces, Carole, now eleven, and Linda Gail, now eight, had essentially become my younger sisters.

Carol and Linda Gail

During the previous year at Thornwell, I had completed the ninth grade, and in the fall began the tenth. After arriving in January of 1952, Helene enrolled me in the tenth grade at Mulberry High School.

At Thornwell, I had played both 'midget' football and a month or so of varsity football. In keeping with my adventurous nature, I decided to try out for basketball, a sport I had never played. On the first day of practice the coach gathered the potential players, gave us basketballs and told us to practice dribbling and take shots at the basket. After a moment, he called me and another kid over, handed the other kid a ball and told me my job was to prevent the kid from taking a shot and to try to take the ball away from him.

A Road Trip

While attempting my assignment, I wrestled the ball away from him. The coach blew his whistle and shouted, '*Foul!*' I knew nothing about fouls. The coach motioned me over and said, '*Listen kid, the wrestling coach should show up any moment now. Why don't you meet with him?*' The school didn't even have a wrestling team. I didn't need that coach's sarcasm; I needed encouragement.

During the winter, I didn't participate in a team sport. Instead, I spent after school hours working with Richard at the grocery store, feeling mostly bored and restless. In the spring, I joined the track and field team as a runner.

Our team was so small I had to train for both the four-man medley and the mile race. I preferred the mile, and in one race, I 'broke five' (running a mile in less than six minutes).

At one track-meet, the events took place in a stadium with a quarter mile track around a football field. I was running the mile race. In my third lap of this four-lap race, some ten yards ahead of the competition, my coach sent a team member to the side of the track to tell me to slow down and save some energy for the medley race taking place later.

There were spectators in the stands cheering for their individual schools. There was no way I was going to slow down. As far as I was concerned, they were all cheering for me. I kept my pace and crossed the finish line well ahead of the other runners. Just beyond the finish line, I saw my coach waiting. I was hoping he would congratulate me, but his facial expression indicated otherwise. He took me aside and said, '*McCabe, what you did was selfish. You have much to offer our team, but you need to become a team player.*'

I felt ashamed and was more cooperative in future races.

Fortunately, we won the medley race. Summer came, and I wanted to avoid working in the grocery store. I found a part-time job ushering in a movie theater in Bartow. I bought a used motor bike (a bicycle powered with a gasoline motor, no driver's license required) and rode it every day, ten miles one way to Bartow. Two months into my job, the motor bike was using so much oil I had to junk it. I went back to working in the grocery store with Richard.

Helene and Richard always gave me lots of freedom and seldom questioned my activities. They appeared to trust me, and I had no intention of disappointing them. As far as I was concerned, Helene was my adopted mother. She was a thirty-two-year-old mother of two girls while I was barely sixteen. Carol and Linda Gale treated me like I was their big brother.

Richard cared deeply about his community. He was an active member of both the Lions Club and the American Legion. He also helped coach little league base-ball. He usually spoke softly and seldom passed judgment on others. He was a kind husband and father, but seldom demonstrated affection. He was not a hugger, but expressed his love with other actions.

Richard became my father figure. I had the utmost respect for him. When I questioned Richard about his time in the war, he spoke lightly of his experiences, but never provided details of the fighting. I later learned that men who have fought in battle and have seen their comrades die are reluctant to talk about their combat experiences.

In the fall of 1952, I was sixteen and in the eleventh grade. I wasn't satisfied living with Helene and Richard and going to school. I desired something more and was still looking for an unidentified something. I desired to be anonymous, to answer to no one. I was about to make the first of three poor decisions.

On a Friday, in late October, I packed a small bag of clothes, and without telling anyone, I hit the road, hitchhiking west, out of town.

It was midafternoon, and I got lucky, quickly catching a ride to Tampa, then a second ride south, all the way to Miami. There, I spent the night in the bus station. In the morning, a middle age man bought me breakfast. After which he asked me to go with him to his house. I sensed trouble and took off, hustling out of the station, forgetting my small bag of clothes. I walked the streets for a while, then, at a gas station I saw a truck and asked the driver, '*Say, how about a lift?*'

Johnny Age 17

He responded, '*Where you headed?*'

I didn't have a particular destination in mind; I just wanted to get on the road, and ride around the country. '*Jacksonville*' I said. He agreed to give me a ride, and I felt I was off on a real adventure.

I found the world of long-distance truck drivers fascinating. The drivers seldom had to listen to a boss. The world outside was always changing, and I preferred change. These truckers were friendly, and like me, they enjoyed talking.

A Road Trip

My favorite rides were with moving company drivers. Their trailers were filled with several families' furniture and other household goods. They drove long distances and usually stopped to deliver furniture at individual family homes. I helped the drivers unload, carrying boxes and furniture into the house.

The drivers I rode with were kind and generous. When I helped them, they rewarded me with money which I used for food and clothing. The moving-van drivers sometimes needed to add to their load. In such cases, the drivers stopped at storage companies. If their pickup was going to require more than a day, they dropped me at a truck stop where I would seek my next ride.

The tractors had bunks in the rear of the cab where the drivers could sleep when they stopped. Their trailers were seldom totally filled. When they stopped to rest, I found a place in their trailer to sleep. If there was no space in the trailer, I slept on top of it. I recall once sleeping on top of a load of watermelons because the trailer had no top.

Truck stops served good food. They had restrooms where I could wash up. When there was a laundry nearby, I washed my dirty clothes. I felt that someday I might become a truck driver. Much later in my life, I spent a year driving a tractor-trailer to and from Florida and New York.

My First Enlistment

'Life will always be to a large extent what we ourselves make it.' —Samuel Smiles

As of October 1952, I had been on my adventure for three months. I had never contacted Helene or Richard to tell them I was safe.

In December, I turned seventeen, celebrating my birthday somewhere on the road. I decided to visit my sister, Peggy, who lived on Long Island, New York. A driver dropped me off in New York City where I bought a Long Island Railroad ticket to Hempstead. Upon arriving, I called Peggy, and she sent her husband, Paul, to pick me up.

Richard Hawkins Peggy Boyajian Helene Hawkins Paul Boyajian

They were both happy to see me and wanted to hear about my recent travels. Most important, they made me feel welcome.

I had not finished high school, so Peggy and Paul were concerned about my future plans. Peggy offered to enroll me in the local high school, but I declined and told her I might go into the military. Sensing my cavalier spirit, and stubborn attitude, she voiced no objections. I suspect she was relieved.

Peggy was one of my five siblings, but to me she was just another adult. Our personalities seemed to clash. In the end, Peggy and Paul generously invited me live with them until I could decide what I wanted to do next.

My stay with the Boyajian family was a pleasant one. Paul Jr, now five, and his sister, Carolyn, now seven, accepted me as their big brother. When Peggy and Paul were away from home for the evening, they trusted me to stay with their two young children. Paul and his brother Vernon were partners; owners of a discount retail carpet outlet in East Hempstead, Long Island, New York. Most days, Paul took me to his store. He had several employees; carpet installers. I worked as their helper.

One of Paul's employees, Mark, used the company station wagon to deliver carpet. A roll of carpet can weigh several hundred pounds, so handling it was usually a two-man task. I worked as Mark's assistant, riding all over Long Island with him. He had served three years in the Army and was now in the reserves.

My First Enlistment

During our travels he told me about his experiences in the service. Because of Mark's stories, I decided to join the military. I spoke with Peggy and Paul regarding my plans, and they agreed it was a good decision. Eliminate the entire sentence.

Paul treated me like I was a younger brother. He seemed to care about me. Now and again, he sent me on an errand to New York City; usually to deliver a package to his brother, a hotel manager. Paul enabled me to travel and experience sightseeing in the big city.

I was seventeen and attempted to enlist in the US Coast Guard. Like so many males, I was partially colorblind and failed the eye exam. I next applied to the Air Force, and they accepted me. My physical exam took place in New York City at the Whitehall Street recruiting station.

After being sworn in with several other recruits, we traveled by bus from New York City to Sampson Air Force Base. Sampson was located in upstate New York on the eastern shores of Seneca Lake, a few miles south of Geneva. We spent twelve weeks learning the ways of military life. The Air Force called it Basic Training; we called it Boot Camp. I went through basic training with two dozen guys in a group designated with a flight number. We lived together in a two-story barracks and spent many hours each day marching.

We learned to spit shine our boots and to respond loudly, '*Yes, sir!*' and '*No, sir!*' to the TI (technical instructor) who was in charge of our flight. We also cleaned the latrine and had KP duty. KP stood for "kitchen patrol." It was not a patrol at all, but duty that started at 4:00 a.m. and consisted of working in a large dining facility, serving food to thousands of recruits, washing a hundred table tops, scrubbing hundreds of pots and pans and mopping thousands of square-feet of flooring.

During basic training I also learned to fire an M-1 rifle, dig a fox hole and to put on my gas mask while walking through a building filled with tear gas.

After six weeks, our flight was given a weekend pass and allowed to leave the base. I took a bus to the town of Geneva. On Saturday night, I got totally drunk, slept on a park bench and woke up the next morning with my first hangover. I thought, *I'm becoming a real man.*

We young recruits were also given lots of tests to determine how the Air Force could best use us. I hoped to get an exciting job. Perhaps I could work in a control tower and tell pilots when and where to land. Or better yet, I might get to test-fire aircraft guns. But the Air Force didn't need me for an exciting job. They needed aircraft mechanics, and my test results suggested I might be useful as such.

On the day my flight completed basic training, we participated in a multiflight parade, performed in front of a viewing stand. This event was followed by a meeting where we boot camp survivors were informed of the work we would be doing, as well as our training assignment. I was to receive training as an aircraft mechanic at Amarillo AFB in Texas.

Those of us assigned to Amarillo were bused to Syracuse where we boarded a C-47, an airplane nicknamed the Gooney

Bird. This was my first time to fly, and I had mixed feelings about this form of travel. I was concerned the plane might crash, but I felt excited about seeing the earth from high in the sky. The C-47 did not have pressurization, so it had to fly below ten thousand feet. The flight was bumpy. Like several other Airmen on the plane, I got airsick and had to use a barf bag.

On our way to Amarillo, the plane made a refueling stop in Indiana. As it neared our final destination, I had my first view of the dusty Texas Panhandle. It looked like a desert, flat with very few trees, and the wind was blowing sand everywhere. I had never seen such land, not even when I was riding with those truckers. Most of us trainees were from the East, so once we were on the ground, we just stared at the great space all around us.

A military bus took us to our new home, a large two-story barracks. It was an improvement from the one we lived in during basic training, with a common room containing a pool table and a ping-pong table. There were other airmen there, who were already in one or more training phases. Those who had just arrived were to wait weeks before their training began.

Each day, those not in training were assigned to "police" some area of the airbase. To police an area means to pick up trash and cigarette butts, a boring and disgusting task. I was seventeen years old and about to make a stupid decision.

Henry and I had gone through basic training together

and were both given the same training assignment. I had sat next to him on the flight to Texas. We were scheduled for training in the same flight and had to wait. I was bored and restless. Henry was homesick. On several occasions we discussed leaving. I told him how easy it was to hitchhike, so one evening we left the base.

It was dark when Henry and I walked across several large and dusty fields, searching for a highway. In the morning we hitchhiked east on US Highway 66, heading for Oklahoma City. After arriving, Henry took a bus to his home in Indiana, while I continued hitchhiking further east. I never saw Henry again.

It was late June 1952, and my first destination was South Carolina, where I hoped to see my first girlfriend, Verna. She had graduated and was waiting at Thornwell before leaving for college. We had not kept in touch, but she had been on my mind.

I carried my military duffle bag but never wore my military uniform. I was AWOL from the Air Force and feared they were looking for me. The closer I got to Clinton the more excited I became. It was late in the afternoon when I arrived there. I walked to the Thornwell campus and met some kids who remembered me. They told me where I might find Verna. Making efforts to avoid any of the adults, I eventually caught up with her.

Verna was residing in the Home of Peace. We planned a late-night rendezvous. Around midnight, I snuck into her building, then into her bedroom and then into her bed. As the night came to an end, we both realized we were not in love.

The meeting was our last intimate encounter. I began to recognize there is a difference between mutual need and mature love. As for maturing, I had a long way to go.

The next morning, I was leaving, but I didn't have a specific destination in mind. Leaving Clinton, I simply traveled in the direction opposite from where I had come. I let my hitched rides determine my destination. I had come from the South, so I hitchhiked north.

The lack of money became an issue, so my next stop was in Ohio, where I got a job on a farm. It came with a wage, as well as a room and meals. The work was uninteresting. I lasted about two weeks. I traveled next to St. Louis, Missouri, where I landed a job with the Union News Company, selling candy and newspapers on passenger trains that traveled in and out of the city. The company gave me a badge to wear. I rode in the baggage car where I kept my supplies. The company provided sleeping quarters in last-stop towns.

After a week of riding trains, I quit, but kept the company badge. As long as I rode in a baggage car, the badge continued to afford me free rides on trains. No one ever questioned me or asked to see my ticket.

My last free train ride was from Chicago to Boston. That was an overnight trip, so I slept in the baggage car. For some reason, I desired a specific destination and decided to travel north to Machias, Maine, where I was born. From Boston, there were no trains traveling north, so again, I traveled by way of my thumb.

Arriving in Machias, I visited a library. I wanted to find out if I had any relatives in the area. Finding a lady librarian, I explained that Machias was my place of birth and asked her if she knew any one with the last name McCabe.

The librarian told me there was a Barbara McCabe who had married a Mallar. The librarian told me Mrs. Mallar lived on Center Street, across from the cemetery. Locating the house, I introduced myself and discovered Mrs. Mallar was my Aunt Barbara.

I was unaware of any family members still living in Maine. Barbara was my father's cousin. She told me that my father's mother was still alive and living in Machias in a boarding house. Barbara told me where I could find my grandmother McCabe. I had no memory of her, but located her and visited with her for about an hour.

She had lost some of her abilities to speak clearly, so I failed to understand much of what she said. Of her six grandchildren, I was the only one she saw after our family left Maine in 1936. Grandmother McCabe died a few months after my visit.

After leaving Machias, I made my way to Calais. That was where Mr. Robinson hired me to clean his rental cabins. It was where I had stollen the money and spent a night locked up in the city jail.

During 1952–53, I was incarcerated for nine months

My First Enlistment

and had time to think about my life thus far. I felt stupid for having gone AWOL. I knew the military would eventually find and punish me. I knew stealing from others was wrong. I had been ungrateful to steal money from Mr. Robinson who had given me a job, as well as a room to sleep in and food to eat. I had no excuse for what I had done. My poor decisions had taken me back to where I was born. It was there I had a rude awaking. A criminal at seventeen, I had made a poor start in life. Thus far, I had committed a crime and spent nine months incarcerated. I wondered, where was I headed? At the time, I had no idea that two men, my brother, Buster, and my brother-in-law, Richard Hawkins, were going to help me recover from my poor start in life.

My Second Enlistment

'Life isn't about finding yourself. Life is about creating yourself.' —George Bernard Shaw

In April of 1953, after receiving an undesirable discharge from the US Air Force, I returned to Mulberry, Florida, to live temporarily with Helene, my oldest sister, and her husband, Richard Hawkins.

I was eighteen, and in spite of my earlier history, they were not giving up on me. For a second time, they were extending me help.

My sister, Jean, who was twenty-one and single, lived in nearby Lakeland, working at a local restaurant as a car-hop. She had an automobile, and let me use it to get my driver's license. Richard helped me get my own car by cosigning a loan. I found a job in Lakeland, working for a roofing subcontractor. Earning $1 an hour, I could only afford a room in a rooming house in Lakeland.

During the work week, I survived mostly on peanut-butter-and-jelly sandwiches. On weekends, I stayed with Helene and Richard and enjoyed meals with them. I had a family connection again, and attempted to live independently.

Richard talked with me about getting an education. Mr. Purcell was the Polk County School Superintendent and a friend of Richard. Together, they spoke with me regarding an opportunity to earn my high school equivalence diploma (GED). Mr. Purcell had the authority to award a GED. He gave me a book regarding the economic history of America and told me to meet with him when I was ready for a test.

A month later, Mr. Purcell visited Richard, saw me, and asked if I was ready for my test. I told him I was even though I had only skimmed the book. After work the next day, I met with Mr. Purcell in his office. He asked me a couple of questions, and my answers apparently satisfied him, because he handed me a signed diploma.

Helene reminded me that Granny Leighton had left me some money in a trust fund. Granny had stipulated, until I turned twenty-five, I could use the money only for education. Helene suggested I speak with the admissions people at Florida Southern College located in Lakeland where I was living. The college agreed to accept me provided I did some remedial study in the summer. During the summer of 1953, I took two self-study courses: geometry and reading comprehension. The related tests were easy.

In the fall I quit my job, took up residence in a Florida Southern dorm and attended classes. My college tuition was covered by funds from Granny's trust. I worked part-time for the college to pay for my dorm room and food. In less than a year, I had gone from being a kid with no future to a young man attending college.

In truth, I wasn't ready for college. Academic success requires more than intelligence. I didn't yet have the motivation and discipline required to succeed in college. I performed well in mathematics courses, a subject where I had some natural talent and in a mechanical arts course that required no tests.

When summer arrived, I quit college and talked with Helene and Richard about trying to get more work experience. They suggested I talk with Buster, my brother about getting a job in Philadelphia. Remembering the promise, he had made when he visited me in the Machias jail, I hitchhiked north to Philadelphia, hoping he would help me.

In July 1954, Buster worked as a tech-rep with a company that manufactured impact grinders. He was thirty-two and married to Dottie. They graciously invited me to stay with them until I could support myself. Buster got me a job in the same small factory where he worked. The pay was low, but it was enough to enable me to rent a room. Dottie and Buster made me feel welcomed. I visited with them often, sometimes eating supper with them. I was again getting help from one of my older siblings.

Philadelphia was a great town for music, parks and museums. In December, I turned twenty and was excited about living there and getting to know my big brother. My rented room was in a house very near the University of Pennsylvania where several Penn dental students also resided. I used busses and trolleys to get around the city as well as for going to and from my job.

For some special occasions, Buster loaned me his 1950 Chevrolet Suburban. On one occasion, I thoughtlessly returned the vehicle with the gas tank almost empty. This caused Buster a great inconvenience. He got angry with me, expressing disappointment in my behavior. His reaction taught me not to take his kindness for granted.

During one visit with Buster, he engaged me in a man-to-man talk regarding my future. He expressed concern I had first dropped out of high school. And now, after one year, I had dropped out of college. He suggested I was not yet mature enough for college, and my undesirable discharge from the military would seriously limit my future employment opportunities. He had learned it might be possible for me to re-enlist in the military and asked me what I thought about the idea. I told Buster, *'I would really like to start over.'*

He said, *'Let's go see our congressman.'*

In 1945, William T. Granahan was elected to his first two-year term as a member of the House of Representatives from Pennsylvania's Second Congressional District. He lost the next election, but regained the seat in 1949. He served in Congress until his death in 1956.

Congressman Granahan lived in the heart of Philadelphia. On the evening of January 5, 1956, Buster and I met with the Honorable Congressman Granahan in his living room. Our discussion focused mostly on my past. I expressed regrets for my stupid actions and a desire to recover from my poor start.

My Second Enlistment

Granahan confirmed that it might be possible for me to re-enlist, but the decision would need to come from the Air Force. The meeting ended with the congressman saying he would look into the matter. Could such a meeting take place today in such an important man's home?

On May 25, 1956, Congressman Granahan died, but not before writing a letter on my behalf, requesting the Air Force to consider my request to re-enlist. A second enlistment would enable me to earn an honorable discharge. I felt this goal was more worthy than even a college degree.

In the spring, a letter arrived informing me a military board at the Pentagon in Washington, DC, would review my case at a specified date and time, and I was welcome to attend the review session. I thought, '*Wow! The Pentagon no less, where generals and admirals work, and I was invited to be there!*'

With my invitation in hand, I traveled to DC and found my way to the Pentagon. There, I was escorted to the room where the review board was to meet. I was asked to sit in a chair just outside the closed door. I felt excited about the upcoming meeting.

After a short time, I was invited into the room, where I encountered lots of military brass. They sat at what looked like a judge's bench in a courtroom. From their height they looked down and asked me to state my case. They specifically wanted to know what I had done since my discharge, and why they should permit my re-enlistment.

I told them about earning the GED and my year of college. They wanted to know why I had quit college. I explained how important an honorable discharge was to me. I could always return to college after successfully serving my country. The meeting lasted only a few minutes. Before I left, one of the officers stated they would inform me by mail of their decision.

Weeks later a letter arrived informing me that the review board had decided I could re-enlist in the Air Force. The local Air Force recruiting office was located in downtown Philadelphia. The day after receiving the letter, I called in sick and visited the recruiting office. They were expecting me.

On March 15, I was sworn in and given a train ticket to San Antonio, Texas where, for a second time, I would go through basic training. In 1956, all Air Force basic training was at Lackland AFB, located near San Antonio.

Upon arriving, I was bussed to the base where I met the members of my Flight and our technical instructor (TI). My Flight was atypical because it was comprised of recruits who had previous military experience. Some were enlisting from the reserves; others from the Army or Navy. I alone had re-enlisted after receiving an Undesirable Discharge, a fact I kept to myself.

My goal was to earn an Honorable Discharge. I needed to start a new life where no one was aware of my past. I decided to change my name. Johnny, with an ugly past became Jack, with a promising future. From that time, on I introduced myself as Jack McCabe.

My Second Enlistment

Officially I was John, but to all except my immediate family, I was Jack.

Our flight went through a familiar routine. Our heads were shaved, and we collected uniforms, boots, bedding and a duffle bag. We were given shots, and after receiving a small portion of our first paycheck, we visited the base store to purchase essentials.

Our new home was a two-story barracks where we claimed a bunk. We then spent time with our not-so-friendly TI. As a special flight, we never did KP, we were never gassed and we were never given leave. But we marched and marched and marched some more. And we were tested for our usefulness.

Again, it was not my choice to become a mechanic, but the Air Force had not changed the test. They were determined to turn me into an aircraft mechanic at Amarillo AFB. Our basic training ended after six weeks, and I was given a two-week furlough.

I returned to Philadelphia by bus to visit Buster. He had purchased a Hudson Hornet and gave me his six-year-old Chevrolet Suburban. Perhaps he intended to reward me for starting my recovery. I detested being a freeloader, so months later, I sent him some money from my service pay. He returned it, saying the car was a gift. After all, Buster lived in Philadelphia, the City of Brotherly Love.

My second arrival for training at Amarillo was much different from the first. I was twenty, a bit older than the other trainees, and unlike them, I had a car. Amarillo is one of the cities mentioned in the famous song *Highway Sixty-Six*. I explored that highway and other roads throughout the Panhandle of Texas.

The wind was constant and blew dust everywhere. Every moment I was outside, the sound of the wind was in my ears, an annoying phenomenon. Two dust storms hit the area while I was there. The dust found its way into every living space. No room was spared a collection of very fine sand. The Panhandle of Texas is accurately known as a dust bowl.

The technical training consisted of some hands-on experiences and some theory. It included nomenclature and vocabulary regarding the various systems we encountered. I learned that jet airplanes are powered through space by the thrust from mighty jet engines. When a jet engine is running, you could be sucked into it if you got too close to the front. You could be incinerated by it if you got too close to the rear.

I learned the names of the surfaces connected to the wings of an aircraft. There are flaps, elevators, ailerons and trim tabs. Various parts of an airplane sometimes fail, and we lucky recruits were being trained to make the necessary repairs.

Each week, the other twenty-four trainees in my section and I studied a new topic and completed a related test. I found the material interesting and the tests easy. I finished at the top of my class, an accomplishment earning me a choice for my next assignment: Germany or Okinawa.

Near the end of World War II, American forces landed on Okinawa. It was the last island where US troops confronted the enemy before attacking the Japanese homeland. The battle for Okinawa played an important and costly part in the final stages of the war. The location and history of that small island in the Pacific Ocean seemed a place that promised adventure. Okinawa was my choice.

The Air Force was sending me overseas, so they gave me a three-week furlough. During my leave, I drove to Mulberry, Florida, to visit Helene and Richard. I wore my uniform, and girls in the small town paid me some friendly attention.

Unable to take my Chevy Suburban to Okinawa, I left it with Richard and signed it over to him. Buster's old Chevy stayed in our family until it became junk in 1962.

My trip to Okinawa was going to be by ship from San Francisco. I gave myself ten days to hitchhike from Florida to California. It was an adventure I relished. I hitchhiked wearing my khaki-colored Air Force uniform and carrying my military duffle bag. Gas stations offered sinks for keeping somewhat clean. People seemed pleased to be helping a soldier. Drivers talked to fight boredom and fatigue. Sometimes they asked me to drive, but they never asked me to pay for gas.

Through Tennessee and Indiana, I rode on two freight trains, experiences that involved uncertainties. Hopping a freight train is illegal. You're not sure where the train is headed or when you'll have a chance to safely exit. And you may not be the only one on board.

In a rail yard near Nashville, Tennessee, I spotted some open-door boxcars attached to a freight train. The position of the engine indicated the train would most likely travel north. I crawled into a boxcar and waited. After a while, the train traveled north and then stopped for a time in Kentucky. There, two hobos joined me on the train. At first, I felt a bit wary of these dirty looking characters, but they were more concerned about not getting caught. They warned me to stay away from the open door.

Soon, the train started moving again. The hobos sat at one end of our boxcar drinking something, while I sat at the other end, pretending to sleep. I was tired, but with the hobos nearby, I was much too anxious to sleep. The next time the train stopped, I exited and boarded another freight train standing on a nearby track. I quickly fell asleep. This second train traveled north to Lafayette, Indiana, where I exited and again took up thumbing rides on the highway.

Two young ladies picked me up in Saint Louis, Missouri, and drove me into Chicago where they invited me to a party. I slept on someone's sofa and, the next morning, took a bus to the western suburbs of the city.

My longest ride was with a trucker through Minnesota all the way to central Montana. Somewhere in Montana, I looked across miles of land to distant mountains. The scenery was spectacular. An off-duty state trooper gave me a ride, and went out of his way to drop me at a place where I could get inexpensive lodging. We were in the middle of nowhere, and he reasoned I might have to wait a long time for my next ride. Fortunately, I did not have to stay there overnight. The

My Second Enlistment

next car going in my direction stopped and parked across the street in front of a tavern. The driver was alone and hollered, *'Hey soldier, where're you headed?'*

I hollered back, *'California!'*

He came back with, *'Come have a beer with me. I'll give you a ride to the next town.'* I accepted his offer.

My next ride was with a trucker hauling steel to Spokane, Washington. I rode with him through northern Idaho where I saw many more impressive mountain views. The next evening found me riding, with a family of three beside the Columbia River Gorge toward Portland Oregon.

Two days later, I entered California from the north arriving at Travis AFB, located near San Francisco. There, I learned my ship was a week late. "Hurry up and wait." was a common occurrence in the military. The trip through fifteen states had taken only seven days. Why was this?

I was on the move twenty-four hours a day and often slept while riding. I ate between rides or when my driver stopped to eat. I was never stranded, and the next ride usually came quickly. Unlike American soldiers returning years later from the Vietnam War, I was treated well. As late as 1953, American troops were fighting on the Korean Peninsula. An armistice had been signed, but there remained a potential for more fighting. I was young and traveling in uniform; all of these conditions contributed to my early arrival at Travis.

My successful re-enlistment and basic training encouraged me to work diligently while attending aircraft mechanic school. My goal was to do well at my assignments and to eventually earn an honorable discharge. Success with technical training helped me to overcome my early restless nature and reckless behavior. The Air Force offered me recognition and provided acceptable boundaries. I now felt accepted by my peers and appreciated by my superiors. My childhood search for a vague something was over.

An Island in the Pacific

'Life will always be to a large extent what we ourselves make it.' —Samuel Smiles

For military personnel assigned to serve in the Far East, Travis AFB was a base of departure and return. Today, the mode of transportation into, and out of Travis is usually by air. In 1956, my trip across the Pacific Ocean was by way of an old troop ship, berthed in the San Francisco harbor. With a name I cannot recall, and measuring at over four hundred feet in length, the ship appeared huge.

Together, with some five hundred other servicemen from the Air Force and Army, I carried my duffle bag aboard the big ship. We sailed down the coast to San Diego, where we took on fuel, as well as some Marines. After San Diego, we never saw land again until we docked at a port in Japan.

On board, the enlisted men were quartered by branch of service. Each branch had separate cafeterias, sleeping areas and latrines. My quarters were three floors below the top deck, very near the bow, probably the most undesirable location on the ship. In rough seas the bow is constantly raised by the waves followed by downward plunges, a series of motions causing seasickness. Soon after heading west, the ship hit bad weather, and most of us became sick. We crowded into a latrine located in the bow of the ship. I was one of thirty guys in the latrine and lucky to be standing over a toilet. Others stood at a long trough that served as a urinal. Each time the bow raised, we all retched, and together, produced an unpleasant chorus. I was in too much discomfort to appreciate the humor of the synchronized sounds.

Out on the vast Pacific Ocean, the big ship seemed small. Only when we went topside in calm seas did I experience any pleasant moments. Viewing the sea on a calm and sunny day, I saw a beautiful ocean and flying fish. I too wanted to fly and get away from the dreaded sickness.

Those in charge kept me busy working, sometimes pulling KP duty, washing pots and pans. Experienced sailors working on the ship promised us we would eventually get our sea-legs. After one gets sea-legs, the body adjusts to the motion, and one no longer feels nauseous, even in the roughest of seas.

After many days at sea, our ship stopped briefly at Yokosuka Naval Base in Japan. The Army guys got off, and the ship traveled south to Taiwan to collect more Marines. I acquired my sea-legs on the south bound leg of our journey. Reaching Taiwan, we docked at the port of Keelung, near the city of Taipei. Some Taiwanese came on board to unload. We traded American cigarettes for some beer and other alcoholic beverages.

While at Keelung, more Marines came on board. They

An Island in the Pacific

too were destined to serve in Okinawa. The ship's authorities were notified of a typhoon heading our way, so after taking on fuel, the ship headed back to the ocean. The storm had already produced very rough seas, and the newly boarded Marines were soon feeling the results. Many Marines got sick; too many to fit into their latrine. Some of them had to use ours. I watched those tough Marines suffer, just as we flyboys had. The rough seas spared no one who was not yet standing on their sea-legs.

After seventeen days at sea, the ship arrived at the island of Okinawa, the largest of many in a chain of islands stretching a thousand miles from Japan to the Philippines. This small island is about one-third the size of Rhode Island.

The ship docked near the capitol city of Naha, where I saw a hundred or more Marines standing on an uncovered dock. They were leaving the island, taking our place on the ship. From one of those soldiers, I made a timely purchase: a Cushman motor scooter for $90. I was among the few enlisted men on the island who owned a motorized vehicle.

Okinawa measured sixty-five miles in length and only twenty miles in width at its widest point. I was soon on the road again, riding every mile of the few roads on this small island. Kadena AFB was bordered on the West by a north-south highway running along the South China Sea. One entered the base from the East through the main gate.

Living quarters for enlisted men were two-story dormitories. My dorm contained the Orderly Room (the squadron headquarters) and the office of Colonel Tiger Davis, commander of our outfit, the 67th Fighter-Bomber Squadron. The dorm had a large common room with a pool table, a ping-pong table and some comfortable furniture. On each floor there was a latrine with showers. The dorm windows had metal shutters. They were closed when a typhoon was forecast to hit the island.

Jack at Kadena Dorm on Okinawa

A large cafeteria/dining hall on base provided enlisted men a meal at almost any hour of the day or night. Officers had the same opportunities in a more attractive setting. There was a gym with a large room containing training equipment for physical conditioning. Playing pool was my favorite pastime. Eventually I took up tennis, a sport I continue playing to this day.

An Airman's Club, where I sometimes drank beer, was located across the street from my dorm. On our once-a-month payday, I would go to the club for a dinner of shrimp fried rice, and follow up with a bowl of pineapple ice cream.

The twenty or so pilots in my squadron flew the F-86H jet, a single-seat aircraft used as a fighter/bomber. The F86-H was capable of carrying either a bomb or an external fuel tank under each wing. The aircraft also had machine guns on each side of its nose. They were used for 'dog-fighting,' engaging enemy fighters and for strafing enemy ground forces. The purpose of most flights was for training and maintaining flying skills.

Each airplane was flown by a number of pilots, but was assigned to only one mechanic. He was called the 'crew-chief' and was responsible for maintaining the overall condition of the airplane. He prepared the aircraft for each mission, recorded all maintenance performed on the airplane, ordered new parts, and requested specialists to repair electrical and instrument systems. The position was highly coveted because the crew-chief was entitled to name the plane and to paint that name on both sides of the airplane. Additionally, the crew-chief's name and hometown were stenciled on each side of the canopy.

To earn the position of crew-chief, I had to first work as

an assistant and prove I was capable of such an important assignment. In three months, I went from rookie mechanic to crew-chief. Remembering my first girlfriend from my days at the orphanage, I had the name Verna painted on each side of my airplane. This airplane was also painted with a special stripe on each side because it was flown by Colonel Davis, the squadron commander.

Jack in Cockpit of Squadron Commander's F-86

Early morning flights were common. On those days, I was up by five, finished breakfast by five thirty, and on the flight-line servicing my plane by six. The pre-flight inspection had to be completed by the time Colonel Davis arrived for his scheduled seven o'clock takeoff. The servicing and inspection tasks involved refueling the airplane, topping off engine oil and hydraulic fluid, and checking tire pressure.

On a military combat aircraft there are various safety pins. Some are installed to prevent the landing gear from collapsing; others prevent the pilot's seat from accidentally ejecting.

After Colonel Davis was seated in the cockpit, he started the jet engine and I removed the pins. I disconnected the power unit (an external source of electricity), removed the entry ladder and pulled the wooden chocks from under the wheels. Standing in his view, I used hand signals to signal all was ready. The plane then taxied to the runway and took off.

Around two hours later, Colonel Davis would return and again need hand signals as he endeavored to park the plane. He would enter the revetment (a parking space protected by sand bags) and swing the plane around so it was pointed in its original position.

After he shut down the engine, I chocked the wheels, installed the safety pins, positioned the entry ladder and connected the power unit. Colonel Davis reported any system malfunctions, and I wrote appropriate notes in the aircraft's maintenance log.

One Sunday afternoon, while returning on my scooter from an outing in the countryside, I came across an American Army officer standing beside his stalled car. I stopped to help and discovered he had a clogged fuel line. I was able to clear the line and get him on his way.

The Army officer sent a letter-of-appreciation to my squadron commander, Colonel Davis and to the 18th Wing

Headquarters. Several days later, Master Sergeant Payne requested I meet him in his office at Wing Headquarters.

In 1953, Sergeant Payne had been stationed at Amarillo AFB, the same time I was there in the stockade. He had worked in personnel at Amarillo and was now the highest-ranking enlisted man at Kadena. He was aware of my past history as well as the letter from the Army officer and had decided to submit my name for Airman of the Month.

Airman-of-the-Month was an honor given by Wing Headquarters to one airman in recognition of a job well done. I felt I had performed no better than any of my fellow crew chiefs and suspected the award was an acknowledgement of my recovery from my ugly past. The sergeant explained I would be interviewed by a selection committee and suggested that for the next few days I read the *Stars and Stripes*, a newspaper printed daily by the military. Knowing what the committee would ask, he told me to get caught up on current events. I followed his suggestion, and during my interview, I was able to answer each of the current-event questions.

A week later, Colonel Davis informed me I had been chosen as Airman-of-the-Month. He told me I could take two weeks and travel anywhere in the Far East where the Air Force flew. He suggested I visit Hong Kong, a city where he had recently visited and had purchased some suits. He gave me the name and address of his tailor in Hong Kong and suggested the man might be of some help in this foreign city.

I couldn't afford a tailored suit, but I was excited about

visiting Hong Kong. After arriving there, I found my commander's tailor. I introduced myself and he told me Colonel Davis had sent him many customers. I explained I could not afford a suit, but was hoping he might suggest an inexpensive place where I could stay.

The tailor smiled and showed me to a small room in the back of his shop containing a bunk bed. He explained he had an apartment upstairs, and that I could sleep on the bunk. It was a gracious offer, and I slept there each night I was in Hong Kong.

Following my week in Hong Kong, I flew by military aircraft to Tokyo. Twelve years earlier, Japan and the USA had been at war. In 1958, I found the Japanese people friendly and accommodating.

I wanted to visit Mount Fuji. A Japanese gentleman, who spoke English, helped me purchase a ticket and directed me to the correct train. The overnight trip ended at the base of Mount Fuji, a most impressive sight. After my visit to Japan, I returned to Kadena.

Back in Okinawa, I learned my squadron was due to exchange our F-86H Sabre fighters for a newer airplane, the F-100D Super Sabre. We anticipated their arrival with excitement. One day, we all watched as four new fighter/bombers flew over the base, kicked in their afterburners and entertained us with some impressive flying. I was among the first mechanics assigned as a crew chief on one of those planes.

In 1953, the United Nations and North Korea signed

an armistice, specifying neither side would introduce new weapons. While I was at Kadena, the North Koreans began flying a new Soviet Mig fighter aircraft near the 38th parallel. In response, my squadron was chosen to spend a month on temporary duty (TDY) flying the new F-100s over the same skies. My flight to South Korea included a scary moment.

F-100 Super Sabre

There were eight of us mechanics flying in a C-119, Flying Boxcar, loaded with lots of support equipment. Arriving over our refueling site in Japan, word came from the pilot that our plane was low on fuel. He had only one chance at a safe landing. If he could not land the plane on the first pass, we were to bail out.

There was a sergeant on board who served as the loadmaster. If we had to bail out, it was his job to get us out of the plane. We all wore a parachute. This one chance at landing resulted in the sergeant ordering us to stand up and hook our parachutes to a strap attached to a rail on the ceiling of the plane. He explained our chutes would open as soon as we exited the airplane. He went on to say if the chute didn't open right away, we should pull the rip cord that dangled in front of the chute.

As the plane lost altitude and the landing gear descended, I felt the initial stages of panic. I was located at the end of the line and had no desire to bail out of the plane. When the sergeant came to check my equipment, I shouted, '*Sergeant, I don't think I can jump. I'd be happy to remain on board and stay with the pilot.*'

The sergeant loudly replied for all to hear, '*If anyone of you rookies hesitates, the copilot and I will shove your ass out the door!*' I was standing and clutching tightly to a nearby large piece of equipment, my knuckles turning white. Fortunately, the plane landed safely, and I felt a great sense of relief.

During our month in South Korea, it was winter, cold and icy. Before each flight, we used large heaters to melt ice off the wings of our new airplanes. Our one-story open barracks was heated by a coal-burning stove, needing hourly attention to keep it hot. When our time of duty was up, I was pleased to get back to the tropical conditions of Okinawa.

Back in Okinawa, I enjoyed going to the shores of the South China Sea. My buddies and I found outcroppings where the waves crashed against and washed over large rocks. These places provided access to the deep water we sought for snorkeling and diving. Floating on the surface of the clear water, I saw fish swimming thirty feet below me. Diving down and returning with a speared fish was an exhilarating experience.

When not on duty at the base, my Cushman Scooter

allowed me to visit small villages in Okinawa. I encountered friendly natives and observed their simple farming lifestyle: no beggars, only happy children and smiling adults. They all seemed content in this faraway world. I traveled roads providing views of both the Pacific Ocean and the South China Sea. One view was a reminder of the horrors of war.

In the summer of 1945, when American troops landed on Okinawa, Japanese soldiers refused to surrender and convinced the civilian population that American soldiers were barbarians. More than a thousand Japanese women and children jumped off seaside cliffs, committing mass suicide along with the soldiers. Looking over one cliff, I saw what looked like bones below. I felt sad for the Japanese soldiers who were denied life in a new and more prosperous Japan.

After two years in Okinawa, the Air Force assigned me to Homestead AFB, located twenty-five miles south of Miami, Florida. Before I left the island, I sold my scooter for $90, the same price I had paid for it two years earlier.

Traveling on a military transport service (MATS) airplane, I flew from Kadena to Tokyo, Japan. A day later I flew from Japan to Hawaii with a brief refueling stop at Midway Island. Five years earlier I had flown on a C-47, an aircraft called the Gooney Bird. On Midway, I saw lots of real Gooney birds dancing. On Hawaii we had a day to visit Honolulu, then it was on to Travis AFB in California.

An Honorable Discharge

'All's well that ends well.' —Shakespeare

Leaving Travis, I enjoyed another trip across America, hitchhiking from California to Florida. Hitching rides east, I traveled through Reno, Nevada, where I spent a brief time at a gambling table. I also spent a night in Las Vegas. In both cities, I lost enough money to learn that the odds are stacked against most novice gamblers.

In Oklahoma City, I caught a ride with two women, a mother and her daughter. The daughter was in her late twenties. I did most of the driving as we traveled to Panama City, Florida. We were together on the road for three days. Each night they paid for my motel room.

After arriving in Mulberry, Florida, I spent a few days visiting with my sister, Helene, and her husband, Richard. They told me they were proud of my recovery from the undesirable discharge and my progress toward earning an honorable discharge. Richard helped me buy a 1945 Ford, which I drove to Homestead, my new duty station.

My squadron at Homestead was part of SAC, the Strategic Air Command. The famous General Curtis Lemay served as commander of SAC. The year was 1959, and Dwight Eisenhower was President. On Okinawa, as a crew chief on a fighter aircraft, I had worked mostly alone. At Homestead, I worked as a member of a team, maintaining a B-47 bomber. I found teamwork much less motivating, but I was on my way to achieving my goal of earning an honorable discharge.

At Homestead, I found excitement, hitching rides on KC-97 refueling missions. The pilot of a KC-97 was the man in charge, so I always found him when seeking approval for a ride. They usually allowed me to join them on local training missions. The crew of six consisted of four officers—the pilot, copilot, navigator, and radio operator—as well as two enlisted men, the flight engineer and the refueling boom operator. The crew was a team, and at any given moment, each member contributed information essential to the mission.

While riding in the back of the KC-97, I studied the boom operator. He released the boom and it hung below the tail of the tanker. As a B-47 slowly approached the boom, I looked out the operator's window and saw the bomber's pilot.

The boom operator guided the end of the device into an access hole near the nose of the B-47. The two aircraft flew connected while fuel was pumped from the KC-97 into the B-47 at the rate of 5,400 pounds per minute. After only a few minutes, the boom disconnected and the bomber slowly dropped back, banked to the right and disappeared from my view.

Flying high over Florida, I enjoyed viewing the land and

coastlines of the state. At twenty-three, I really enjoyed flying in those military airplanes. Now, sixty years later, I hate flying with commercial airlines. I really miss those early years!

I was in the US Air Force, stationed at Homestead Air Force Base, located some 30 miles south of where the three ladies lived. Another airman at the base was dating one of the nurses. He arranged for me to have a blind date with Ellie. Upon arriving at the apartment, I met Ellie. But I also met Loretta. I had one date with Ellie, then, during the next day, I called the apartment and asked to speak with Loretta. She agreed to a date, and that was the beginning of our love affair.

Like all young couples falling in love, we spent our free time together, talking about what our lives had been before meeting. We began to understand each other, made love quite often and enjoyed visiting interesting places throughout the Miami area. We visited several beaches, one in South Beach where the adjacent hotels were constructed in the art-deco style. Months later we decided to get married.

In September of 1959, Loretta and I were married. She had lived with her parents in Westminster, Maryland, graduated from high school there and then became a nurse after attending a nursing program at Union Memorial Hospital in Baltimore. She, along with two ladies in her nursing program, moved to Miami, FL. The three shared an apartment near Doctors Hospital in Coral Gables, where they all worked.

Loretta's family was Catholic, so the marriage ceremony took place at the Catholic Church in Westminster. In attendance was Loretta's extended family and three of my five siblings, Buster, Helene and Peggy. This was the first time that we four siblings had gotten together since I was in the orphanage. The only thing that would have made it better would be if my other two siblings, Jean and Joan, had been there with us.

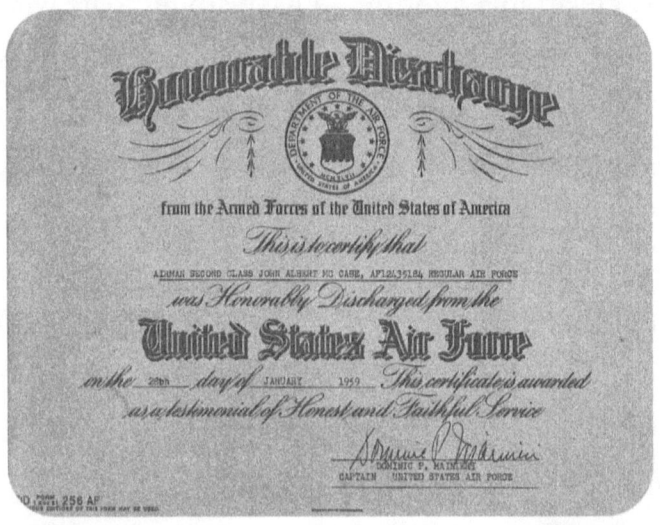

The four of us spent time talking about our parents. It was during our conversation that I first leaned that our mother had inadvertently caused her own death by attempting to abort her pregnancy. This was also the last time we four siblings were together.

Loretta and I returned from Maryland and rented an apartment in Coral Gables, FL. Loretta found a job as a nurse, and I continued serving my country at the base in Homestead. During this time, Loretta became pregnant with Jackie, and I began earning college credits.

An Honorable Discharge

I started taking after-hours college courses offered through Florida State University. Our teachers were officers stationed at Homestead, and our classrooms were located on the base. I enrolled in every available course and earned several college credits.

My math teacher, Captain Williams, a military lawyer, worked in the Homestead AFB Judge Advocate Office. I excelled in his class. He took an interest in my future education, and made me aware of another way of earning college credits.

The United States Armed Forces Institute (USAFI) originated in 1942, as a wartime service for Army enlisted personnel. It provided those soldiers an opportunity to continue their college education. Eventually, USAFI services were extended to all military servicemen, enlisted and officers alike. During the time I was taking college courses on the base, I also enrolled in several USAFI correspondent's courses. Each course ended with a test. I scored well enough to accumulate several more college credits.

During the summer of 1960, I had earned a large number of college credits. Master Sergeant Price was the highest-ranking enlisted man in my squadron. He became aware of my desire to earn a college degree and arranged for me to serve a special duty, a position enabling me to continue toward my goal. Sergeant Price assigned me to work in an underground building at the end of the runway.

Since 1950, the United States and the Soviet Union had

been engaged in a Cold War. Homestead AFB was one of several bases where the Air Force had planes on alert for instant response to Soviet aggression. For twenty-four hours, I was on duty with several other mechanics. After our duty was completed, we were off for forty-eight hours.

There were four bombers loaded with nuclear weapons parked nearby. While on duty, we mechanics performed only one task. Upon hearing the Klaxon horn, we rushed as fast as possible to our assigned B-47 and helped prepare the plane for takeoff.

There were lots of drills, announced at random times. No matter what we were doing—sleeping, eating, or bathing—upon hearing the alarm, we rushed to our assigned plane. It was guarded by an armed airman holding a leash attached to a German shepherd guard dog. More than once I rushed to my airplane wearing only my undershorts.

Arriving at my plane, I quickly started an external power unit, removed various safety devices, and assisted the crew as they climbed aboard the bomber. After each of the engines were running. I disconnected the power unit, removed the wheel chocks, and signaled the pilot that the plane was ready for takeoff.

During one drill, I saw a totally naked mechanic running to his plane. A picture of the mechanic approaching the airplane and the growling dog would have been a great Kodak moment.

The twenty-four-hours-on followed by forty-eight-hours-off enabled me to attend classes at the University of Miami. The college campus was only twenty miles north of the base. I enrolled in math and physics courses.

My first course in calculus was taught by Professor Herman Meyer, a mathematician who looked much like Alfred Hitchcock. For students encountering their first experience with calculus, Professor Meyer had created a unique approach to this abstract subject. He explained complex concepts using non-jargon language. His course and teaching style inspired me to choose mathematics as my college major. I excelled in his class, and he suggested I consider graduate school after earning my Batchelor's Degree.

Captain Williams was aware that I was accumulating college credits. He told me about Operation Bootstrap, a program sponsored by the military in partnership with Florida State University. The program enabled active servicemen to complete their final year of college on the FSU campus. By May of 1960, along with those few credits earned earlier at Florida Southern College, I had accumulated enough college credits to apply for the FSU program.

One day in early June, Captain Williams called me into his office and handed me new orders, assigning me to attend classes at FSU. Loretta and I moved to Tallahassee, Florida, and I began my senior year of college.

Florida State University is located in Tallahassee where Loretta and I lived in an off-campus apartment. She worked as a nurse while I attended classes. Loretta, pregnant with

Jackie, spent most of the summer (too hot and muggy in Florida) at home in Maryland with her family.

To earn enough credits to graduate, I enrolled in classes during the regular 1960–61 school year as well as during both summers of 1960 and 1961. I majored in mathematics and minored in physics.

Two of my classmates in a math course were Army officers in graduate school studying meteorology. They needed to learn calculus and, because I spoke up a lot in class, they thought I could help them understand the material. Though I was an enlisted man, these officers sought my help, which I proudly provided.

In August, Loretta returned to Tallahassee in time to attend my graduation. Helene and Richard were also at my graduation where I was awarded a bachelor of science degree. Both of them had helped me recover from my disastrous youth, and expressed pride in my accomplishment.

Loretta and I returned to Homestead where we lived in a downtown apartment. I continued my duties as an airman at the nearby Homestead Air Force Base. My work consisted mostly of refueling aircraft at night. In November of 1961, Captain Williams, now Major Williams, called me into his office and congratulated me on earning my college degree. He explained that I could not apply to officer's candidate school (OCS) because I had been convicted earlier of a crime involving moral turpitude. He then told me I would get an early discharge if I could land a job teaching math in a

An Honorable Discharge

public school. I asked, '*Would it be an Honorable Discharge?*' He replied, '*Yes.*'

In 1957, the Russians had launched Sputnik, and the US government was determined to train more engineers and scientists. In 1960, John F. Kennedy became president. His administration decided the country needed more science and math teachers. Any enlisted man who could obtain a science or math teaching position was eligible for an early discharge.

I wanted out of the Air Force, so I sought the assistance of a local employment service, asking them to locate a math teaching positions. They discovered a position in Baltimore County, Maryland, starting in January the next year.

The person to contact was Mr. Vincent Brandt, Math Supervisor for Baltimore County Schools. I had my college transcripts sent to him. He called and interviewed me over the phone. During our conversation, I learned that Mrs. Betty Hitchcock, head of the math department at Milford Mill High School in Randallstown, Maryland, was six months pregnant and needed to go on maternity leave at Christmastime. Her replacement would cover her classes through the remainder of the year. Hitchcock was to return the following September. After hearing the description of the position, I explained, '*Mr. Brandt, I didn't major in education, and I have never taught school.*'

He responded, '*You can always take education courses at night and in the summer. Your transcript indicates you have taken more mathematics courses than the typical high school math teacher. The position is yours if you want it.'*

On December the 6th, 1961, Jackie was born at the base hospital at Homestead AFB. A month later, I received an Honorable Discharged from the Air Force. While Loretta and Jackie were flying home to Westminster, I was driving north to the same destination. Our family of three lived in an apartment on Green Street in Westminster, and I was a math teacher at Milford Mill High School, located west of Baltimore near Reisterstown.

My first enlistment in the Air Force had ended with an Undesirable Discharge. A year later I had been given the opportunity to start over. I had re-enlisted with very little education but with a goal to earn an Honorable Discharge. I now had an opportunity to return to civilian life with both an Honorable Discharge and a college degree. I accepted Mr. Brandt's offer.

On January 16, 1962, I received an honorable discharge from the US Air Force. I felt proud at having recovered from my youthful mistakes. And I was very excited about becoming a math teacher.

Success and Failure

'In school, you're taught a lesson and then given a test. In life, you're given a test that teaches you a lesson.'—Tom Bodett

I entered the teaching profession with no formal training. In college, I majored in math and minored in physics. My teenage life included very little time in public schools, but I felt confident I could rise to this new challenge. I also planned to teach only until the end of the school year, and then get a 'real' job in industry.

Milford Mill High School served a large Jewish community. These families placed a high value on education. Their teenage children were motivated and were enrolled in high level math courses. I encountered these bright students the first time I taught math.

My teaching position began in January, the middle of the 1961–62 school year. My students missed their absent teacher, Mrs. Hitchcock. She was an accomplished math teacher with an excellent reputation, so I had big shoes to fill. My first challenge was to win them over; to convince them I was worthy of being their teacher.

I was able to get their attention by telling them I had never finished high school and was coming to them from the military. They questioned, *'How could this be?'*

I told them a little about my life in the orphanage and that I had dropped out of high school and joined the Air Force. I did not tell them about my criminal past. After explaining how I had earned a GED and went to college while I was in the service, they seemed relieved.

Every new teacher must pass their students' testing. The challenge was to become the leader of this bright group of teens without becoming their 'enemy.' Fortunately, my sense of humor and my knowledge of mathematics were enough to earn some credibility. In the Air Force, I was a low-ranking recruit, but in the classroom, I was in command, responsible for the progress of each student. I felt like a master sergeant and enjoyed the experience. I decided to give the profession a further try.

In 1964, I applied for a grant from the National Science Foundation to attend a Master's Degree program at Rutgers University in New Jersey. The grant I was awarded paid both tuition and a stipend that came with campus housing. So, after two and a half years at Milford Mill, we moved to New Brunswick, NJ, the location of Rutgers.

The mathematics program included several advanced math courses. They were both engaging and challenging. My favorite class was Algebraic Geometry, taught by Professor Rafael Artzy. During my year at Rutgers, Artzy was offered

Success and Failure

a Full Professor position at SUNY Buffalo. Upon earning my Master's degree from Rutgers, he asked me to join him at Buffalo, where I would enroll in a PhD program and earn a salary as an Instructor.

Some of my undergraduate students were attractive females. I began secretly sleeping with one, then another. I became an unfaithful husband. Thinking back on my dishonest behavior, I try to understand why I wanted to be free from the limitations of married life. I cared about Loretta and Jackie, but became confused regarding what I really wanted from life. Before me were exciting opportunities accompanied by feelings of guilt. How could I leave a loving wife and a precious daughter?

In the orphanage and in the military, I was bound by institutional life. Being married is also a set of boundaries. I wanted to be free to explore life outside of these limitations. I was acting selfishly. My need for something unrestricting was stronger than my feeling of guilt. I began an on-again-off-again relation with my wife and daughter.

During the Christmas break, I drove our family to Loretta's parent's home for a two-week visit. When it was time for me to return to Buffalo, Loretta and Jackie did not accompany me. Loretta never questioned my intentions, and I never brought up the subject. We both had ambivalent perceptions regarding our future relationship. I knew Loretta loved me. She hoped I would regain the feelings I had for her.

Back in Buffalo, I lived alone while finishing the course

work required by the PhD program, achieving all but writing a dissertation. My sponsoring professor, Rafael Artzy, took a position at Temple University located in Philadelphia. He invited me to join him there, where I was to work with him and write a dissertation. I returned to Loretta, and we moved to an apartment in Abington, Pennsylvania, located a short distance north of Philly.

While we lived in Abington, Loretta worked as a nurse at a local hospital, and I taught evening math courses at Temple. Artzy had arranged for this position enabling me to earn a salary. My part-time students were adults. They had fulltime day jobs and attended college in the evening courses while attempting to earn a degree. Again, I secretly slept with some of my female students.

After a year at Temple, I failed to write a dissertation and took a teaching position in 1969 at Stetson University in DeLand, Florida. Loretta, Jackie and I lived together in a house near the ocean in Ormond Beach. When Jackie was six years old, she attended first grade in a local elementary school.

In January of 1970, while attending a math conference in New Orleans, I met John Myhill. I had encountered Professor Myhill two years earlier at SUNY Buffalo. He had been my teacher in courses on Mathematical Logic. Myhill asked if I had written a dissertation. When I informed that I had not done so, he offered me a paid research position back at Buffalo. He was giving me another opportunity to write a dissertation. After four months at Stetson, and with the approval of the head of Stetson's Math Department, I returned to SUNY Buffalo with Loretta and Jackie.

Arriving in Buffalo, I desired to live alone, so Loretta and Jackie lived in an apartment several miles from the university campus. I was Jackie's weekend dad. I attended several advanced courses regarding mathematical logic, but failed to find a topic to focus on. My research position ended in July. I desired to remain in Buffalo, and took a one-year teaching position at Rosary Hill College located in nearby Amherst, NY.

After two years in Buffalo, I returned to DeLand, FL, and to my position as an Assistant Professor at Stetson. I had failed to make any progress toward a dissertation. Loretta remained in Buffalo, where she worked as a nurse and raised Jackie. I made several trips to Buffalo to visit with Jackie. Although Loretta and I eventually divorced, she has always been kind to me. Later, Loretta and Jackie moved back to Maryland. When Jackie was in 5th grade, she visited me in Florida.

In 1974, after failing to write a mathematical dissertation, I lost my position at Stetson and drove a truck for a year. I once drove my tractor-trailer through Maryland, where Loretta allowed Jackie to accompany me for a week. When she was 13 years old, she visited again and attended my wedding to a woman named Margaret.

Jackie, Age 7

I loved Jackie, but I was not in her life when she needed me, and for that, I was a poor father. Additionally, I never sent money to Loretta to help her raise my daughter. As her absentee and un- supporting father, I lost a chance to form a deeper bond with Jackie.

Searching for My Parents

'The most important thing that parents can teach their children is how to get along without them.'—Frank Clark

I have often wondered how different my life would have been if I had known my father and mother, and had felt their love and support. I'm sure my relationships with individual men and women would have been different. The man who came closest to being my Dad was my brother-in-law, Richard. He was my oldest sister's husband (see chapter with title A Road Trip, page 40.)

In the orphanage, I was not well liked by the other boys. I wasn't bullied, just unpopular, usually the last one selected in pick-up games. Because these boys did not seek my friendship, I had low self-esteem. Not by choice, I was a loner.

My military experience forced me to encounter small groups of men, some older and more mature than I was at the time. With some of my peers, I was completely at ease. Developing a friendship with some individuals was easy. Gaining entry into a group was impossible. Something in my early personality was off-putting to my peers.

When I was sixteen, riding around the country in trucks, I enjoyed the company of the adult drivers. To earn their friendship and attention, I always offered to help them load and unload their trailers, treating them as I would a father.

One time on Okinawa, I organized an off-shore visit to a nearby small island for a group of seven other airmen. I was twenty-one at the time, and I had discovered that we could pay a local native Okinawan to take us in his small boat to a nearby island. On this much smaller island, populated with only a few families, we hiked around and found military artifacts from World War II. And we drank lots of beer. The adventure was entirely my idea, and its success gave me a sense of the skill and responsibility required for leadership.

My talent for mathematics also provided me with leadership opportunities. I served as Head of Math in three different high schools and as an Assistant Principal in another high school. These positions provided opportunities to mentor beginning teachers and to counsel experienced teachers. I admired the successful leaders I served under. While working with my supervisors and leaders in education (and for a short time in private industry,) I always desired to earn their respect while hoping they would earn my loyalty.

Not until I was thirty, did I experience significant friendships with other men. While in graduate school at SUNY Buffalo, I met two other guys who were also working toward a PhD in mathematics. We three spent a lot of time hanging out together and enjoying each other's company. The sense of belonging to this small group was a new experience for me. It fostered my self-esteem and aided my maturation. I began to like who I was, and to enjoy myself. I still had a long way to go towards fully accepting who I was. Not until I was sixty, did I feel comfortable hugging another man.

When I retired at age seventy-nine, I moved to a 55-and-older retirement community in Florida. I had coached high-school tennis for many years, and was still an avid player. I met another retiree who played tennis five out of seven days a week, provided weather permitted. He is ten years my junior. Ever since we met on a tennis-court, he has been a very good friend; in many ways a soul-mate. I have learned to depend on him when I need help. He could never be my 'Dad', but he is what I admire in a man: honesty with integrity, consistent, mentally healthy and dependable. After back surgery in 2015, I can no longer play tennis, so he and I now compete at pool tables.

With men, I had never expressed my feelings or emotions. With women, it was the very opposite. I became sexually active at fifteen.

My first time was with a fourteen-year-old girl at the orphanage. Since those early years, I have always been attracted to women. When I began a relationship with a woman, I needed to trust her with my most intimate thoughts. For me, an emotional component was a prerequisite for intimacy, a need that is probably related to the absence of a mother in my early life. I sought a very attractive woman, one who was highly intelligent, and one with whom I would have good chemistry. These requirements limited my search.

I was married twice, the first was with Loretta. Our marriage ended after only seven years. Even though I married Loretta when I was twenty-three, I was too immature to know how to sustain and nurture our relationship. Then, for nine years I was single and enjoyed several intimate relationships. I was searching for the 'ONE.'

In January, 1975, I married Margaret. We were both in our second marriage. My daughter, Jackie was barely in my life, while Margaret was already raising three children from an earlier marriage, two sons age seventeen and thirteen, and a daughter age nine. Margaret had graduated Summa-Cum Laud from the University of Colorado, majoring in Biology. Her dad was an Engineering Professor at the university.

For the most part, her children accepted my role as their step-father. Disputes were rare, and never with her older son. Our marriage lasted thirty-two years. Margaret died in 2007 at the age of seventy-three.

In 2008, I went on-line with E-Harmony, again hoping to find the 'ONE.' In addition to my requirements, I also limited my choice to women ten years my junior. Almost immediately, I found Sharon. I was attracted to her high spirit and wonderful smile. She had recently divorced a very controlling and unfaithful husband. Her situation was challenged her to rediscover herself. She needed to learn how to make decisions that effected only herself. Her son and daughter were already high achieving adults. During our relationship, I attended both of her children's wedding.

Sharon lived in Annapolis, Maryland, while I was residing in New Milford, Connecticut. Most weekends, I drove or took the train to Annapolis, visiting with her at her home there. One summer, we traveled together, visiting the Galapagos Islands. We took two trips to visit her sister in Rochester, New York, and made several trips to enjoy the culturing offerings of New York City.

We were sharing some wonderful moments together, but we were also having serious disagreements. We both eventually discovered we were seriously incompatible. For example, I desired to take month-long cross-country camping trips. But for Sharon, a long-distance drive was a three-hour trip to a Holiday Inn, and camping in the woods was for scouts.

Sharon also enjoyed a good argument, while I avoided conflicts. I was crazy about Sharon, and for the most part, I really liked being with her. For me, Sharon would be high-maintenance. We eventually both came to the same conclusion. We could be good friends, but we could never live together. To this day, we have humorous phone conversations every two weeks or so, sharing the happenings in our individual lives. Sharon, by far, came the closest to being the mother I had always been searching for.

A Life with Mathematics

'Young men should proof theorems, old men should write books.' —G.H. Hardy

When I was in sixth-grade I found I was better than my peers at learning math. In grades nine and ten respectively, I excelled at Algebra I and Algebra II. After mastering arithmetic, the properties of algebra made perfect sense. I quit school during grade eleven.

While attempting to earn a PhD in math at SUNY, Buffalo, I was introduced to the Foundations of Mathematics and Mathematical Logic, two subjects in which I found interest. As I indicated earlier, I never wrote a dissertation and failed to earn a PhD.

My failure to write a dissertation is difficult to explain. Contrary to Artzy's and Myhill's perception of my talent for math, I had little faith in my ability to find and solve an original math problem, one deemed worthy of a dissertation.

To write a mathematical dissertation, one must select a current topic, then study everything that is known about the subject. This research is supposed to lead one to an open question. One would then need to be first to discover an original proof regarding some nontrivial truth about the open question; a proof that would add only a tiny piece to some esoteric puzzle.

I did not have the interest, confidence or discipline required to begin such a challenge. Furthermore, neither of Artzy nor Myhill suggested a dissertation topic. I suspect they thought I could find a topic all by myself.

From a book I received while I was at Temple University, I taught myself how to create computer programs with Fortran, a programming language created for engineers. I developed algorithms and wrote computer programs to execute these algorithms. One algorithm could produce prime numbers, (2, 3, 5, 7, 11, …) and another could express a number into its prime factors, e.g., 5,803 = 13*17*23.

What I really wanted to do was to prove an ancient conjecture regarding even numbers. This mathematical conjecture was posed hundreds of years ago, and is easily understood by high school students. In spite of the incredible evidence supporting this proposition, it remains unproven to this day.

The proposition, known as Goldbach's Conjecture, states that each even number larger than 6 equals the sum of two distinct prime numbers. For example, 5,804 equals the sum of the two prime numbers 103 and 5701. Whoever proves the conjecture will become instantly famous and join the likes of Euclid and Einstein.

I developed an algorithm and a corresponding computer

program to find the two prime numbers for a given even number, hoping this this mathematics would lead me to a proof of Goldbach's Conjecture. Even though I failed to discover a proof, it was a labor of love, and inspired me to self-publish three books on the topic:

Numbers Galore: Perfects, Primes, Triples and Twins, Discoveries in a Playground of Numbers, Exploring Numbers with Python.

These books are available on AMAZON.

The Beginning of Thornwell Orphanage

'Generosity during life is a very different thing from generosity in the hour of death; one proceeds from genuine liberality and benevolence, the other from pride or fear.' —Horace Mann

Thornwell Orphanage opened its doors on October 1, 1875. The institution was the brainchild of William Plumer Jacobs, a Presbyterian minister of a small church in Clinton, South Carolina. Jacobs's mother died when he was three, and his grandmother, on his father's side lost both her parents. She was adopted by William Plumer, a Presbyterian minister in Richmond, Virginia. Jacobs's father named his son in honor of the adopting minister.

While living in Charleston, young William regularly walked by an institution known as the Orphan Asylum. Perhaps the early death of his mother, the orphaned grandmother and the images of the Orphan Asylum, together, inspired the young minister to start an orphanage.

In April of 1864, William, a recent graduate of the Columbia Seminary in Columbia, South Carolina, accepted a position to preach in churches in Duncan's Creek, Shady Grove and Clinton. All three churches were located in small communities in South Carolina. The Civil War was underway. For medical reasons, William was unable to join his southern compatriots.

In May of that year, Dr. William Jacobs was ordained and installed in the church at Clinton. As Clinton's Presbyterian minister, Jacobs's major concern was the small size of the town. He hoped the population would increase when the war ended.

In honor of his favorite theology professor, Jacobs named his orphanage Thornwell. He wanted his orphanage to be unlike the regimented institutions of the past. Jacobs envisioned small cottages where homeless children experienced early life in a manner similar to children living in a middle-class family. Each child was to reside in a cottage with a matron or a married couple, who was to provide a homelike environment.

Soon after the war ended, Jacobs married Mary Jane Dillard. They were unable to find a matron for his first cottage, so William and Mary Jacobs moved into the Peace Cottage, becoming its first house parents. There, they cared for their own two children and the original nine orphans. This cottage eventually became the Home of Peace.

Five years after Jacobs established his orphanage, he founded Clinton College which eventually became Presbyterian College.

Reflections

'Life will always be to a large extent what we ourselves make it.' —Samuel Smiles

My young rebellious nature was the root of my early uncooperative behavior. But this temperament also enabled me to acquire the confidence to survive some of life's challenges. Though I was an orphan, I never felt poor. At Thornwell, I received care, and had experiences that taught me the value of work. But I seldom felt loved or appreciated by the adults at Thornwell.

Today, school guidance counselors help teenagers cope with life's challenges. Not so in my time at Thornwell. But then, not every teenage kid is lovable. I needed to constantly test the limits of my boundaries. I was rebellious and stubborn, and the adults at Thornwell were unprepared to deal with a confused teenager.

During those repeated escapes from the orphanage, I was unaware that I was looking for some nebulous thing; roots perhaps, or acceptable constraints. If I had I stayed at Thornwell and graduated, I would have had an opportunity to go to college. I wasn't thinking about the future; my needs were 'now.' I was immature and failed to recognize what Thornwell had to offer. With help from my brother and brother-in-law, I eventually survived my teenage years.

My brother Buster an I never developed a really close relationship. He was more like an uncle who understood and un-judgingly accepted my youthful errors.

He took my recovery as a matter of fact. Buster died in 1965 at the age of forty-four.

My brother-in-law, Richard, was born in 1916 and was more like a father to me. He too understood and un-judgingly accepted my early mistakes. He always seemed pleased that I returned to the Air Force and earned an Honorable Discharge. He loved life and worked until the day he died, in 1980.

Both my brother, Buster, and my brother-in-law, Richard, trusted and encouraged me. Their timely actions of support and guidance made all the difference for me as I attempted to recover from the mistakes of my youth. I can still feel their unspoken love, and they will always be in my heart.

I am now eighty-five and have learned many lessons while getting to this age. Most important, I learned happiness is a state of mind and developing a positive attitude is the best medicine for unhappiness. Life has been good to me, and I have often felt I was in the care of an angel assigned to look over me. I have often been impatient, undisciplined, and impetuous. My angel worked hard, and the adventures have given me wonderful memories. Good memories are the rewards of growing old.

Reflections

My fifty-year career in education brought me many years of happiness and moments of joy. My students' achievements led me to believe I was an effective teacher.

Teaching was like serving as a tour guide in a math museum, moving from topic to topic, helping students experience the beauty and power of mathematical thinking. Challenged to convince students that mathematics is relevant to their future, teaching always included salesmanship. Many of my students had little early success, and they were convinced they could not do math. This required me to act as a coach and counselor. My challenge was to help them each discover their unique talents and values. As a teacher, I enjoyed all three roles: tour guide, salesman, and coach.

A Letter to My Great Granddaughter

'Be yourself, everyone else is taken.' —Oscar Wilde

February 28, 2021

Dear Olive:

Today, you were born in the early morning, during a full moon. Welcome to America and Planet Earth. I wonder how old you will be when you read this letter from your Great Grand-Dad.

Your mother, Jennifer, is my grand-daughter. Your grandmother, Jackie, is my daughter. She was born when I was married to Loretta, your Great-Grandmother.

Olive, my purpose for writing you is so you can learn some things about your mother's side of your family. When Lorretta was much younger, she lived with her parents in Westminster, Maryland. She graduated from high school and then became a nurse after attending a nursing program at Union Memorial Hospital in Baltimore. She, along with two ladies in her nursing program, moved to Miami, Florida.

The three shared an apartment near Doctors Hospital in Coral Gables, where they all worked.

I was in the US Air Force, stationed at Homestead Air Force Base, located some 30 miles south of where the three ladies lived. Another airman at the base was dating one of the nurses. He arranged for me to have a blind date with Ellie. Upon arriving at the apartment, I met Ellie. But I also met Loretta. I had one date with Ellie, then, during the next day, I called the apartment and asked to speak with Loretta.

She agreed to a date, and that was the beginning of our love affair.

Like all young couples falling in love, we spent our free time together, talking about what our lives had been before meeting. We began to understand each other, made love quite often and enjoyed visiting interesting places throughout the Miami area. We visited several beaches, one in South Beach where the adjacent hotels were constructed in the art-deco style. Months later we decided to get married.

Loretta's family was Catholic, so the marriage ceremony took place at the Catholic Church in Westminster, Maryland. She was twenty-two and I was twenty-three. In attendance was Loretta's extended family and three of my five siblings, Buster, Helene and Peggy. This was the last time we four siblings were together. My siblings have now passed on.

Soon after the wedding, Loretta and I returned from Maryland and rented an apartment in Coral Gables, Florida. Loretta found a job as a nurse, and I continued serving my country at the base in Homestead.

Back in 1954, I had started working on getting a college education, but I wasn't really ready for college. I lacked the motivation and self-discipline required, so I joined the Air Force. In 1959, while at the air base, I began again to earn college credits, some at the University of Miami. This was the time Loretta became pregnant with Jackie. Earning these credits eventually led to my earning a Batchelor Degree from Florida State University, studying mostly math and physics.

On December the 6th, 1961, Jackie was born in the hospital at Homestead Air Force Base. A month later, I received an Honorable Discharge from the Air Force. While Loretta and Jackie were flying home to Westminster, I was driving north to the same destination. Our family of three lived in an apartment on Green Street in Westminster. I was a math teacher at Milford Mill High School, located west of Baltimore near Reisterstown.

After two and a half years we moved to a house in New Brunswick, New Jersey, where Rutgers University is located. At Rutgers, with a grant from the National Science Foundation, I enrolled in a Master's Degree program in math, and graduated in August of 1965. We then moved to Buffalo, New York, where I took courses required for a PhD in Math at SUNY Buffalo.

Olive, I wish I could tell you we all lived happily ever after, but real life is more complicated. Each of us live with our short comings and imperfections. At the university, I was both a graduate student and an instructor. Some of my undergraduate students were attractive females. I became an unfaithful husband.

Thinking back on my poor behavior, I try to understand why I wanted to be free from the limitations of married life. In the orphanage where I was raised from the age of four, as well as in the military, I was bound by institutional life. Being married is also a set of boundaries. I wanted to be free to explore life outside of these limitations. I was acting very selfishly. My need to be free from these boundaries and limitations was stronger than my feeling of guilt.

During the Christmas break, I drove our family to Loretta's parent's home for a two-week visit. When it was time for me to return to the university, Loretta and Jackie did not accompany me. Loretta and I both knew our marriage was on shacky ground. I knew she loved me and hoped I would recapture the feelings I once had for her.

While Loretta lived with her parents, I lived alone in Buffalo, finishing the course work required by the PhD program. I achieved every requirement except the writing of a dissertation. My sponsoring professor took a position at Temple University located in Philadelphia. He invited me to join him there, where I was to work with him and write a dissertation. Loretta and Jackie joined me, and we moved to an apartment in Abington Pennsylvania, located a short distance west of Philly. While we lived in Abington, Loretta worked as a nurse at a local hospital, and I taught evening math courses at Temple. My sponsor had arranged for this position that enabled me to earn a salary. These part-time students were adults who had fulltime day jobs and enrolled in evening courses. With two of my female students, I was again an unfaithful husband.

While at Temple, I failed to write a dissertation and took a teaching position in 1969 at Stetson University in DeLand, Florida. We three lived in a house near the ocean in Ormond Beach. Jackie was six years old and attended first grade in a local elementary school. After four months at Stetson, I was invited to return to SUNY Buffalo, where I was given another opportunity to write a dissertation. Arriving in Buffalo with Loretta and Jackie, I desired to live alone, so they lived in an apartment several miles from the university campus. I was Jackie's weekend dad. After two years in Buffalo, I returned to DeLand and to my position at Stetson. Loretta remained in Buffalo, where she worked as a nurse and raised Jackie. I made several trips to Buffalo to visit Jackie. Although Loretta and I eventually divorced, she has always been kind to me. Eventually, Loretta and Jackie moved back to Maryland.

In 1974, Jackie lived with my family. Margaret and I married on January 1, 1975, and Jackie attended our wedding. She also attended fifth grade for a short time in a school close by, where Margaret was a teacher. She eventually returned home to her mother in Maryland.

When Jackie was thirteen, she ran away from home and I found her staying in a half-way house in Daytona Beach,

Florida. She stayed with my family until Margaret could no longer tolerate Jackie's behavior. I faced a difficult decision. Jackie could live with me in an apartment or I could send her back to her mother. I now wish I had tried to raise Jackie, but at the time I decided it was best to return her to her mother. Failing to write a mathematical dissertation, I lost my position at Stetson and drove a truck for a year. I once drove my tractor-trailer through Maryland, where Loretta allowed Jackie to accompany me for a week.

Olive, I want you to know I loved Jackie and still do. I was not in her life when she needed me, and for that, I was a poor father. Additionally, I never sent money to help raise Jackie. As Jackie's absentee father, I lost a chance to form a deeper bond with my daughter. On many days, I feel sad that I lost a great opportunity.

I first met Jennifer, your mother, when she was two years old. Her parents, Jackie and Donnie were visiting my wife and I in Florida. We had a condo at the beach near the inlet in New Smyrna Beach. I remember seeing Jennifer standing in a cardboard box, chewing on the edge of the box. Perhaps she was teething. As she was growing up, I would visit Jen and her mother, Jackie, and her father, Donnie. The four of us would go out for supper, often at a Red Lobster restaurant. Over time, I got to know Jennifer pretty well. She would tell me about her current boyfriend. We talked about her school, the classes she was taking and her teachers.

I was able to attend Jen's graduation from high school.

A Letter to My Great Granddaughter

After the ceremony, the family had a celebration dinner. Along with her parents, Jackie's brother, Sonny, and her two sisters, Karen and Eddie, I too was invited to attend the party. I was so proud of my granddaughter's success.

Your mother attended college in New Mexico, a long way from her home in Maryland. I was living in Florida, but during her Christmas breaks, Jen would fly home and I would drive to Maryland and visit with her and her parents. After college, Jen moved to California.

In 2005, I flew to Australia. While there, I had a heart attack and flew back to the States. After the plane landed in Los Angeles, I had another heart attack. I called Jen and Jackie and they both helped me meet with a heart doctor. The doctor advised surgery, after which I stayed at Jen's apartment in Santa Monica, CA. Although, Jen had just gotten a new job, she would dress my wounds each morning before going off to work. She helped me recover from surgery. You can see, Olive, why Jen and I became close friends. I love your mother very much. I'm now eighty-five, and hope to live long enough to meet you.

During my lifetime I have witnessed many changes: changes in the way people communicate and changes in the way we listen to music. Automobiles, kitchen appliances and home entertainment have all gone through changes, mostly due to advances in electronics and computer technology.

When I was young, letters were composed by writing on paper, using pen or pencil. We wrote using cursive, and sent letters using the US mail. Homes had an ice-box, and ice was delivered from the local ice-house. Each morning we found a newspaper and a bottle of milk on our door step. We listened to music on am-radio (amplitude modulation) and heard loud stereo-music played on boom-boxes broadcast from fm-radio stations. Fm was short for frequency modulation.

We eventually watched sit-comes on black and white television. Television stations ceased broadcasting at midnight after showing the American flag during the playing of the National Anthem. In school we used dictionaries and encyclopedias. When we turned eighteen, we learned to drive cars. Everyone had to learn to shift the car's gears using a clutch. This was before cars had automatic transmissions and turn signals. To inform the cars driving behind, we used hand-signals: arm and hand straight out for left turn, straight up for right turn and straight down for stopping.

When I was ten years old, the phone number at the orphanage was 78. To reach this number you first reached CENTRAL, where an operator made the connection by plugging a wire into a receptacle at a machine where she worked. A long-distance call cost money, but you could attempt to call COLLECT. If successful, the person you were calling paid for the call. Telephones went though many changes. In the seventies, one could purchase a car-phone. I now call your mother using my cellphone.

We went to outdoor drive-in movies sitting in our car. The movie appeared on a large screen, with the sound delivered on device hung on the car door. At first, these films were in black and white, they eventually were in Technicolor.

Refrigerators replaced the ice-box, Microwave ovens added another way to cook or reheat food. Dishwashers replaced hand-washing and electric blenders and egg-beater replaced a lot of hand stirring.

When cars were invented, almost all roads were unpaved. A few roads in big cities were paved with bricks. Now we have many four-or-more lane roads, and multi-lane interstate highways crisscrossing the nation. The interstate system was started by President Eisenhower in the fifties.

While I lived at the orphanage, our inside entertainment consisted of solving picture-puzzles, reading comic books and playing board games like checkers or playing card games like rummy. Before I reached my teens, my most precious possession was an am radio. In my bed at night in South Carolina, I would listen to faraway stations. I remember hearing stations in New Orleans, Del Rio, Texas, and WCKY in Charlotte, NC. Young people today play electronic games on something called Xbox, about which I know nothing.

Our outdoor play consisted of cops-and-robbers, cowboys-and-Indians and team sports like softball. We also had access to swings, sliding boards, see-saws and a jungle-gym. A jungle-gym was a large collection of attached metal bars on which we climbed. Some of us had a bicycle we could ride.

Olive, you were born in the United States of America. Because you and your parents are Americans, you have precious freedoms; freedoms that citizens in some other nations do not have. These freedoms were guaranteed by our constitution, a document that is constantly being re-interpreted.

During the years 2020 and 2021, the world suffered from the covid-19 pandemic. This virus interrupted our normal lives. Our selfish and arrogant president caused damage to our Capital and endangered our Constitution. It appears we have survived the pandemic and the threats to our freedoms. I can only hope that you will enjoy these freedoms for your entire life.

Sincerely,
Your Great Grand-dad Jack

PS: At first my name was John and people called me Johnny. I eventually changed my name to Jack. If you read my autobiography, *Unspoken Love: An Orphans Journey*, you will learn when and why I changed my name.

About the Author

Jack McCabe began a teaching career in 1962. He retired in 2014. He taught mathematics at several universities, including Temple University in Philadelphia, Pennsylvania and Stetson University in DeLand, Florida. He served nine years as head of the mathematics departments at Mainland High School in Daytona Beach, Florida, and nineteen years as head of math at Canterbury School in New Milford, Connecticut, a private prep school

Jack served for five years as a district-level administrator with the Volusia County Schools in Florida and then four years as an assistant principal at Deltona High School in Volusia County, Florida.

Jack also worked in private industry for two years as a computer programmer, first at Continental Testing Labs in Casselberry, Florida, then with NCR in Dayton, Ohio. Before this variety of jobs, Jack served six years in the US Air Force. At seventy-nine, he retired from teaching and now resides in the Villages, Florida.

Appendix

Centuries ago, Euclid proved indirectly that there is no largest prime number. In 1742, Christian Goldbach conjectured, without proof, that every even number greater than 2 can be expressed as the sum of two prime numbers. For example: 100 = 3+97 as well as 11+89, 17+83, 29+71, 41+59, 47+53. I will prove Goldbach conjecture using mathematical induction.

The set of prime numbers is infinite. We can express this infinite set as a sequence of numbers. The next prime number after $P(N)$ is expressed as $P(N+1)$. The sequence of prime begins with 2, 3, 5, 7, 11, 13, 17, 19, ..., so $P(6) = 13$.

We need a process that determines if a given odd number is a prime number. The definition of a prime number requires that a number is a prime number if it has no prime divisors. For a given odd number, we need to check if the number is divisible by any of the odd prime numbers less it. For example, let's determine if 97 is a prime number.

The odd prime numbers less than 97 are 3, 5, 7, 11, 13, 17, 19, 23, 29, 31, 37, 41, 43, 47, 53, 59, 61, 67, 71, 73, 79, 83, 89, 97. Fortunately, we can ignore most of these divisors because divisors come in pairs: (15 = 3*5, 21=3*7, 35 = 5*7, etc.) The largest possible pair is 7*13 = 91. In general, the largest prime factor of a number will be less than or equal to the square-root of the number. The square-root of 97 is 9.848…, so, we conclude that we need only check the divisibility of the prime numbers 3, 5, 7, 11, 13.

A calculator easily reveals that 97 is not divisible by 3 or 5 or 7 or 11 or 13. So, we conclude that 97 is a prime number.

How do we find the next prime number? We use the same process to determine if an odd number greater than 97 is a prime number. A calculator easily reveals that 101 is the next prime number.

The process of finding the next prime number after P(N) will begin by determining if the prime number 2+P(N) is a prime number. It makes this determination by checking if the number 2+P(N) is divisible by any the prime numbers less than 2+P(N). If not, then 2+P(N) is the next prime number. If 2+P(N) is not a prime number, then add another 2 and repeat the process to determine if this next odd 2+2+P(N) number is a prime number.

Proceeding in this manner, you will have discovered the next prime number P(N+1).

To prove Goldbach's Conjecture, I will define a set F. The set F will consist of even numbers each expressed as the sum of two prime numbers. I will then prove that the set F will consist of every even number greater than 6.

For each prime number P>3, I define a finite collection of even numbers, each the sum of two prime numbers.

For the prime number 5, P5 represents the collection {3+5}.
For the prime number 7, P7 = {3+7, 5+7}.
For the prime number 11, P11 = {3+11, 5+11, 7+11}.

In general, for every prime number P>3, PQ represents the collect of sums P+Q, for every prime number P less than Q.

Let F represent the infinite union of each finite set PQ.

$$F = U_{k=2 \text{ to infinity}} (U_{j=2 \text{ to } k+1}(3+P_j))$$

A partial expansion of the set F is shown below:

F = {(3+5)} U
   {(3+7), (5+7)} U
   {(3+11), (5+11), (7+11)} U
   {(3+13), (5+13), (7+13), (11+13)} U
   {(3+17), (5+17), (7+17), (11+17), (13+17)} U
   {(3+19), (5+19), (7+19), (11+19), (13+19), (17+19)} U
Etc.

I need to show that the set F contains every even number. To this end, I must show that there is at least one even number in the set F. And then show that if an even number E is in F, then E+2 will also be in F.

As shown in the expansion above, the even number 8 = (3+5) is in the set F.

Suppose the even number E is in F, then by the definition of F, E=P(N)+Q(M) for some prime numbers P(N) and

Q(M). Also by definition, E+2 is either [P(N)+Q(M+1)] or [P(N+1)+Q(M)]. Both forms of E+2 are in the set F.

By induction, F contains every even number greater than 6. So, Goldbach's Conjecture is true.

As it turns out, my proposed proof does not satisfy the requirements of a FORMAL proof. A formal proof would require a formulated method of determining the next prime number. The method I have illustrated is a trial an error process, although it certainly provides clear evidence of the truth of Goldbach's Conjecture.

www.ingramcontent.com/pod-product-compliance
Lightning Source LLC
LaVergne TN
LVHW091552060526
838200LV00036B/810